Dr. Vega,

Thank you for
supporting EFY

Clive Marchland

WRITTEN TEARS

The true story of a Polio Survivor

By

Chip Marchbank

Order this book online at www.trafford.com
or email orders@trafford.com

Most Trafford titles are also available at major online book retailers.

Printed in the United States of America.

ISBN: 978-1-4669-0792-8 (sc)
ISBN: 978-1-4669-0794-2 (hc)
ISBN: 978-1-4669-0793-5 (e)

Library of Congress Control Number: 2011962298

Trafford rev. 12/14/2011

 www.trafford.com

North America & international
toll-free: 1 888 232 4444 (USA & Canada)
phone: 250 383 6864 ♦ fax: 812 355 4082

FOREWORD

I've never wanted to be better than anyone,

I only want to be equal to everyone.

Why Write

It's been said that when someone writes creatively on a paper it is a gateway into their heart. I think that is true but there is much more to it. When you make a commitment to write your feelings down, you show much more than just creativeness, you expose yourself to the intended reader.

To me, written words can be my way of crying, and it's true. During the times that I've written about loneliness, sadness, or sorrow, every letter has been a tear. At other times when I've written down colorful true stories about myself, it's to bring laughter. In special circumstances while composing a song, it's been for love.

The most inspirational writing to me is writing songs and poetry for love,and it requires three ingredients: careful thought, caring about what you write, and especially love for whom or what you're writing about. Remember the words don't have to flow, but your feelings should.

So take a chance, I think writing down your inter-feelings will help you open the gateway to your heart, and more importantly nurture your spirit.

Chip

DEDICATION

This book is dedicated to my parents, family, friends and mentors that made my life complete.

Oh yeah, it's also dedicated to anyone who takes the time to read it.

CHAPTER
1

Back on July 28th, 1949 in the Midwestern community of Kankakee Illinois, Earnest Gerald Marchbank Jr. and his wife Opal welcomed the birth of their second child, their first boy, Earnest Gerald Marchbank III. Prior to the baby's birth the couple had a discussion and decided if the baby was a boy, they would give the new born the nickname "Chip" to avoid confusion between father and son. I'm not sure that Opal might not have used the "confusion" issue as an excuse to avoid having to brand the name "Earnest" on their son during his youth.

The first few months of Chip's life were spent living in his grandmother's house in Bradley Illinois, while his father attended the prestigious Chicago Art Institute as a student while at the same time he drove a bus to make money as a husband and a parent. Within a year, the family of four, including Chip and an older sister named Cholly, moved to their other grandmother's house in Alhambra California.

Earnest Jr. also known as Ernie, soon found his niche in life working for a major printing company as a dot etcher, establishing and adjusting the color of magazine pictures. In 1950 as Ernie was becoming more established in his work, he and Opal decided to have another child. It was soon after that their life together would change from what they had dreamed of, to the path that the Lord had chosen for them.

In August 1951 while Opal was in the delivery room, Ernie paced the halls of the hospital when he received the news that their son would not survive. The devastation of the couple was overwhelming. Ernie buried himself in his work and Opal, well she became introverted with the sorrow she felt. Seven months past by and the depression Opal was feeling, deepened and even a move to a new home in El Monte, a suburb of L. A. didn't lessen her pain.

One morning late that August, shortly after the move to El Monte, Chip was showing flu like symptoms. Opal was concerned and took the two year old to the doctor. The physician said "don't worry Ms. Marchbank, it's the flu". The doctor gave Chip a penicillin shot and told her to bring him back the next day. This went on for the better part of a week until one afternoon young Chip called to his mother. She ran into the front room to find him dragging himself across the floor with his arms, unable to stand or walk. Opal quickly telephoned Ernie, who made the 20 minute drive home in what seemed an instant. Opal had arranged with a neighbor to watch Cholly, and together the frightened couple rushed Chip out looking for a hospital and the right answers about their sons' illness. The first hospital they stopped at refused to treat the boy fearing that he may be carrying a contagious virus. Ernie was told to take young Chip to Los Angeles General Hospital where he could receive treatment. As the car raced up and stopped at the doors of General Hospital, the couple sensed that once again they were facing a tragic situation. As they rushed their son into the emergency room, the doctors quickly took Chip away from them and swept him off, leaving no time for goodbyes. Time slowly went by and finally a doctor approached the couple from down a cold, poorly lit corridor. His diagnosis struck Opal and Ernie like a lightning bolt. "Chip has Polio and we don't expect him to live through the night". Crushed the couple fell back into their chairs to wait out the night and see what would follow with the dawn. As the hours slowly moved by, both of them slumped in their chairs silently blaming themselves for the tragedy.

Unknown to anyone but God however; Chip was lying in the emergency room preparing to live. To live a life that would be hard at times, and sad at times, but because of the guidance of God and his parents Chip would become the kind of person that could survive and overcome. In fact, he wouldn't trade his life with anyone. How do I know that's true? Because this is my story and I'm proud to say I'm Earnest Gerald Marchbank III, also known as "Chip".

In Sister Kinny Hospital
1952

CHAPTER 2

I realize that at the age of two years old you don't remember much consciously, but I do have some memories of that time in the hospital as the doctors and nurses scurried around me all wearing gowns with masks, while all I wanted was my mom. Unfortunately my parents weren't allowed to see me and the only way they knew I was alive was when they would hear me crying down the hall. Do you know what makes me sad today? It's realizing that at that same time, in that hospital, my parents were crying too.

As time passed by, my fever broke and the doctors went to my parents explaining to them I would live, but the after affects would not be known for quite some time. They went on to explain that my best chance for recovery would be to put me in the care of the Sister Kenny Clinic where they specialized in post-polio treatment. So within a few days I was in an ambulance with my mom and a doctor heading down the road. I remember looking out the window at the hills we were driving by and saying to my mom, "those are my Jesus'es mountains and I'm going to my new home". I didn't know that what I hoped would be, was not to be. My mom just sat there quietly looking out the window as we drove through the country passing meadows and lots of telephone poles. I was too young to realize that the way we were driving was not the way home. Finally the ambulance came to a place that would remind you of a boy's detention farm. It was probably built way out away from everyone to isolate the polio victims away from the rest of society, just like a leper colony.

When they brought me into the clinic, I recall being in a large room with many children in it. The walls were completely tiled from ceiling to floor, it was cold inside and worst of all; my mom was forced to leave. I then was dressed in a gown, placed in a crib with tall metal bars on it, put in isolation and I was afraid and alone. After a few days, I was returned to a room with other children, all of us wondering what had we done wrong.

During my stay at Sister Kenny's, several times each day a nurse would transport me to a large room, she would place me on a bed, and cover my body with hot musty smelling towels. I guess the purpose of the towels was to get my circulation going and to help lessen the affect of the polio virus. A few months into my stay my parents were allowed to visit me for one hour on Wednesday evenings and two hours on Sunday afternoons. That was the limit of contact I had with the outside world.

As the months went by, the paralysis I had suffered in my trunk, arms and legs started to subside, and I was slowly gaining back their use. At that same time I was building a terrible dislike for apple juice and oatmeal, the two mainstays at the clinic. Towards the end of my stay at Sister Kenny's, on Sundays when my parents came to visit, they were allowed to wheel my crib outside into a grassy area. Sometimes my sister and my grandmother would come and peek through the outside fence, and I would catch a glimpse of them. Every Sunday when my parents came, I would rummage through my mother's purse looking for gum or candy. Then I'd always ask, "Do I get to go home today?" It came to a point where my parents hated to come because it hurt them to hear me ask that question, and they in turn would have to say no.

Eleven months went by, and I spent my third birthday in the clinic. On my birthday my parents brought me many presents, some of them were from our neighbors who left them out on the curb because they were afraid to come close to the house.

As the summer of 1953 was ending and fall approached, the day was coming when I would leave the clinic. Maybe I wasn't physically perfect, I had permanent paralysis in my right hip and leg, but I was going to live and I was going home . . .

Home with crutches and leg brace
1953

In 1953 I was finally going home after a one year hospital stay. I really don't remember much other than the leg brace I wore on my right leg and the crutches I had to use. I thought I would only depend on them for a short time, just until I got my strength back.

Little did I know I would never return to what is considered to be "physically normal". For a long time my mom and dad never let on that I was going to be different than other children, and honestly, I didn't think about it. Later, in my adult life, my parents told me that when I was leaving the hospital they ask a doctor if they should treat me differently than the average child. The doctor replied "let him be a boy and don't treat him differently. He will fall and hurt himself, and sometimes other children will make fun of him for trying to fit in as a normal kid, but please don't fight his battles for him, because it will put him in a wheelchair with little desire, drive or commitment to live".

Life really began to clarify at age 4 as I would struggle to adapt to play and be part of the neighborhood kid's society, while living with the physical restrictions that was apparent to all but me. Often times the other children would laugh and mock me, but I was determined to find a way to succeed. I didn't find out until later in life that often my dad would tackle my mom at the front door of the house because she wanted to go outside and chastise the neighborhood children for treating me so unfairly and mean. I'm so glad my father did that, because it molded me into whom I am today. One who believes in proving I can adapt and achieve anything I want if I put my mind and heart into the effort.

I was now approaching the age of 5 and things were once again going to change dramatically in my life. My family was picking up and moving to East Whittier California. There for the next 20 years of my life, I would be sculpted into a strong caring man by the ups and downs, the positive and the negative, the joys and the sorrows that came my way because of my desire to just be treated as a "normal person".

At that time I couldn't have imagined with all the triumphs and tribulations that I was about to have happen in my young life, I would be strengthened far beyond my limits from Polio. I would develop into a leader of men and in the long run, I would discover God had much bigger plans for me.

CHAPTER
3

Truly my first full memory of my life began when we moved to Bogardus St. in Whittier California in the early summer of 1954. Our brand new house was to become my haven when I had to recover from some type of corrective surgery or therapy that doctors would recommend I have. Behind the house was a lemon orchard that became my storied forest where I could go battle dragons, fight wars and always come out the winner.

Soon after we moved into our house, the Wilson family moved in next door. The family was made up of a mom, dad, and three sons. The first day I met the boys they were standing in the back of a pick-up truck. One of the older brothers whispered something to the youngest one. I remember I was standing by the back of the truck with my hand on the tailgate and the youngest boy walked up and stomped on my fingers. I guess they wanted to prove something, but to this day I don't know what it was. Oh well, as time went on we became best of friends.

Although I was wearing a brace on my leg from age 3, it was when we moved to Whittier that I became aware of the significance of it. Let me stop for a moment and explain what this brace was, because it was a big part of my young life. Most of you reading this have probably seen the movie Forest Gump and you may remember him running in leg braces while he was being chased by bullies on bikes. Just before the bikers caught him, the braces explode off his legs and he ran off. Well forget it, polio leg braces were so restrictive not even Superman could have forced them to break. The one that I had to wear had steel bars that started just below my hip, extended down both sides of my leg to the knee where it was fitted with a metal locking hinges on either side and it then continued down both sides of my calf with similar bars that were attached into a shoe locking my ankle in a set position. The brace was held in place by the shoe, a circular strap that went around the top of the thigh and another one across the front of the knee that limited any movement of the leg from the hip down. As funny as it sounds as restrictive as that brace was, it gave me freedom to go out, play and be a boy.

As that first summer progressed I became accustomed to the neighborhood and although I was different the Wilsons accepted me as a friend. Sometimes other kids would come to play with the Wilson boys and I'd hear them say "we don't want to play with the cripple or your little brother Dave, so they would l leave us and the two of us became best friends. Dave was always loyal to me even when it wasn't popular with his brothers and the other kids.

During the time I was adapting to the new living environment, and at the same time trying to prove myself to the kids on my street, I was about to get my first big lesson on cruelty. Although my parents never sheltered me, I was not prepared for what happened with the trials and tribulations of kindergarten. I believe the senseless spitefulness and cruelty of misinformed young children toward a disabled individual can be attributed to the fact that they have not been exposed to the situation and they are intimidated by it. No matter what the reason, summer was ending, school was starting and I was about to deal with it firsthand.

Riding up a winding road into the La Habra Heights and seeing the school out the bus window was my first impression on Hacienda School. It had single story buildings with a large grassy playground around it. Half way across the playground was a large slope that was shaped like a swelling wave and it ran all the way across the field. As the bus pulled into the front of the school and the kids were jumping off the bus, I remember holding up the kids behind me because I had to grab the rail in the bus to get down to the ground because of my brace. The kids were yelling at me to "get out of the way crippled boy". It hurt me to hear that because I was moving as fast as I could. It's interesting because after that first day, and until this day, I always wait to get off a bus, plane, boat or amusement ride last. It's hard to imagine it all started because of comments made in Kindergarten.

Going into the classroom and sitting down at one of the small school desk that were all lined up in a row was an interesting experience. The leg brace, as I described before, had locking hinges on both sides at the knee. When I would sit down, I would have to feel for the lock releases through my pant leg, juggle them until they would separate, and then I could bend the brace to a sitting position. This was not an easy feat under a small desk with other kids going down the aisles and yelling at you to "get your leg out of the way". Throughout all the years that I wore a brace, that's one nuisance I caused that I couldn't correct and unfortunately one other kids never tolerated very well.

During those early months at Hacienda School from time to time my mother would come to the school and pick me up. Just recently she reminded me of a particular day when she pulled up to get me I had tears in my eyes. She asked me, what's a matter? I told her the other kids don't like me, and they won't play with me. My mom said son everyone loves you. I said "mom don't you know, I'm a little crippled boy". It hit my mother hard, because my family never used that term, ever.

My outlook on life was now changing. I wasn't ever going to be considered "normal", I now knew it and I would have to figure out how to deal with it.

At this point in time, I'm going to encapsulate the years of my life from 5-13. Not that the hurtful remarks of treatment was still not prevalent, but I want to touch on some of the various things that happened during that time that made me who I am.

Most every summer, I would have some type of corrective surgery to improve my walking ability and free me from the restrictive leg brace I wore. I had three surgeries to fuse and stabilize my right ankle, another three surgeries to retard the bone growth in my left leg, and finally a surgery to stop the growth of my left leg. The reason the doctors needed to stop the growth in my leg was so both legs would be semi-equal in length. If you take your arms and put them straight out to the sides and measure from finger tip to finger tip, it is usually with-in an inch of your height. My arm span is 6' 4", and my weak leg was stopping at 5' 9". So, unless I wanted to wear a huge platform shoe, the growth in my left leg would have to be contained at that same height.

Back in the 1950's surgery was much more archaic than today, lot's of blood, swelling, adhesions, pain and surgical supplies were not very advanced. Stitches were put in one at a time, blood was left to pool inside the surgery sight. I remember my doctor telling me when the blood soaked plaster casts would come off, I should go outside and let the sun beat on the scars to speed up healing. It was much different than today.

Once again I need to stop and say something here. While I was writing this book many of my friends told me talk about all the physical pain I've endured because of the multiple corrective surgeries I've had throughout my life, or from the injuries I sustained from crazy things I would attempt to do. Here's the deal, when you grow up dealing with physical and overwhelming psychological pain, you learn to mask it. What might be considered excruciating pain for others; I put out of my mind and pretend it isn't there. Mind over matter as they say and you get use to it.

One very nice thing came out of those very early surgeries though, it prompted my parents to put a permanent swimming pool in the back yard for me to rehabilitate in. I spent many hours swimming in that pool healing my joints but more important it was strengthening the rest of my body.

Part of the upside concerning all of these surgeries is I became very proficient on crutches. I could walk, run or balance without using my feet while using them. Back in the 1950's, all crutches were made out of wood, there were no aluminum ones. One year, after one of my surgeries, I was outside on my crutches playing Hide and Seek with the other neighborhood kids. I went to run across the street to tag the "free tree" when I stumbled. I put my crutch out to catch myself and it splintered into large multiple pieces. Some of those pieces skewered up into my arm pit. I don't recommend wood splinters in the old arm pits, they hurt more coming out than going in.

Surgery one summer confined me to a wheel chair, but I always wanted to be outside. On this one particular day, my parents wheeled me out to the front yard to visit with the neighbors. I was holding a baseball bat while I was in the chair and my friends were pitching baseballs to me. One pitch I was thrown I hit right through the large plate glass window of my parents house. I thought they would kill me, but to my surprise they weren't mad, being in that wheelchair was worth something I guess.

One other summer when I didn't have surgery, I was playing over at a friend's house. We were in the back yard and I climbed up on a 6 ft. high fence and fell over to the other side. I heard my arm go crunch and somehow I climbed back over the fence. When I got to the ground, I saw my arm was severely broken. Although the skin was not punctured, my arm looked like an S from the elbow down. My friend's mother placed my arm on a pillow and took me home where my mom immediately rushed me to the doctors where my arm was quickly set. The importance of this incident is not about the injury, it's what happened after that.

Once my arm was set and before the technician came to put on a cast, I remember turning to my mom and saying "Is it alright to cry now?" My mom said "Of course son", but no tears came.

It is important to note that I never have been able to cry. I feel the emotions, but I can't weep and it wasn't until a few years ago when my father passed away that I discovered why. At his funeral I was emotionally destroyed but I couldn't cry. I was sitting with my mother and I turned to her and said "I don't understand why I can't cry". She looked at me and said "I can tell you exactly why. When you were two years old and you were in that hospital, the nurses told all you kids that if you cried they wouldn't let our parents come and see us"; So much for tears!

Anyway I'm digressing; I think you can understand that at a young age many summers were busy but not especially a fun time for me.

One big special event did happen when I was seven. We had relatives out from Illinois visiting and my mom took them to see a live telecast of the game show Queen for a Day. Everyone standing in line was asked to write on a form; if they could be queen for a day, what would they ask for? Everyone was writing long explanations, but my mom wrote six words "cowboy boots on a leg brace". Later she was pulled out of line and made one of the contestants. When it was her turn on the show, she talked about me having had polio and wanting cowboy boots. She won in a land slide and what was amazing to me is that Jack Bailey, the host of the show, knew where to find a place to construct the brace/boot combination before the show ended. That was some accomplishment for 1956.

I overcame a lot of adversities in my young life, but the worst was yet to come. Finding my place in society, discrimination and most important of all, the affairs of the heart.

5th Grade Picture
1959
Between surgeries

CHAPTER
4

L-L-L-O-W-E-E-E-L-L what's that spell? Lowell. Yes that was the name of the brand new high school that opened and I attended my freshman year. My sister Cholly, who was a senior transferred in from La Habra High as well. It was a bright, beautiful and big new school. It was exciting and scary transferring to a place with four times more kids then my junior high. By this time, all but one of my corrective surgeries had been completed, and better yet, my leg brace and crutches were gone. I was a walking machine, although I had a noticeable limp. Running was a different story, I thought I was running but it really was one stride with my weak leg followed by to skips with my good leg. Whether I was running or walking, I would have to use my right hand to put light pressure on the front of my right thigh to lock my leg and foot in place. It is a trait that I still use to this day.

Once again I need to be truthful, at this point in my life I was not a great student. I would rather be playing outside or singing. English, math, or history, I didn't care for. The first semester of my freshman year I tried out for the choir with my sister. We did well, she became the lead soprano and I became the lead tenor. Our choir was only 30 strong, and we had to compete against huge choirs like La Habra High with over 100 voices. I remember in the Orange County Choir Championships our director decided to have our choir sing the Lord's

Prayer in the contest. We ended winning the event. Not only because our little choir was good but we sang the Lord's Prayer in Latin.

It seemed in any direction I would turn that first year, I was challenged and had to try and prove myself. I wanted to take auto shop, I had to prove I had the strength and balance to participate and not get hurt. The other kids didn't have to go through that type of scrutiny. I sought to play sports but was told it's too dangerous for a boy with a disability and immediately shot down. I wanted to play parts in school musicals, but I always had the wrong look (limp) for the part. Mind you I was the lead singing in the choir and you think they would find a part for me somewhere but they never did. My mom reminded me I spent many nights sitting on the front porch of the house praying that I'd get a part in a show, but it never happened. That kind of rejection was very disappointing and it can truly wear you down and it certainly depressed me.

As I mentioned, I also loved to play outside, but the school officials wouldn't allow me to participate in the regular physical education classes, something about safety issues. So, I was put in an adaptive physical education class. This class was held in a gymnastics utility room and consisted of a few kids sitting around playing board games and me. Hanging down from the ceiling was a set of seven swinging rings each of them about 5 feet apart in a straight line. They were situated so you could swing on them starting at one end about 6 ft of the floor and gradually inclined up to where the last one was about 12 ft off the floor. Every day I would swing back and forth across the room on those rings for an hour. The other students thought I was showing off, but in my mind I was flying through the air to another world, a place where I fit in.

Part way into that first semester the adaptive teacher, Bailey Duarte, who was also the high school varsity basketball coach, approached me. He said to me, "Chip, you don't belong in this class. Come and be the manager for my basketball team and you can earn a varsity letter". Having him take me under his wing was a major turning point in my life. As you will see later, it started me on the path that became my future working life, thanks to Mr. Duarte. Anyway, I left the adaptive class and joined up with the basketball team where I was taught and became the official scorer for the team, a trait that followed into my college life. That freshman year the local news papers contacted me and asked me to call in the game summaries and they would pay me five dollars a game. I wasn't going to do it until my father set me down and said; "Son don't miss this opportunity, it's not about the money, it's the learning experience developing your communicating skills on the phone that will serve you well in the future". I took his advice and as always he proved right.

As that year moved bye, I was asked to manage the baseball team and keep their stats for them. The track team wanted my help as well, so it appeared that I was sought after for some abilities, although not on the field. At the end of that first year Mr. Duarte ask me if I knew what Athletic Training was? I said no and he went on to explain it was taking care of injuries to athletes. He then said "I signed you up for a Cramer Summer Course. Take the course, learn and understand it and next year you'll be the trainer for our football team". So I did.

The following fall (1964) it was my sophomore year and I was ready to take on my new responsibility as student athletic trainer. I thought I had learned a lot reading the materials bought for me by Mr. Duarte, but I was far from knowledgeable in the subject. I did show some confidence in what I had learned so people believed I knew what I was doing. The true extent of my knowledge was putting on band aids, tape and elastic wraps, but it helped the coaches and the players too. I went on to be a student trainer until I graduated in 1967 from Lowell.

During that sophomore year I decided to learn to play the guitar and I took lessons at a local music studio. I haven't mentioned this yet but I am 110% left handed and that meant I was going to have to string a guitar upside down and play it backwards to everyone else including the teacher. For some reason it was harder for the teacher to teach then me to learn. I picked up the basic cords and strum patterns and away I went. Not a rock star but pretty good when you throw in my voice. Once again my father wanted me to maximize my abilities so he bought me a very expensive reel to reel tape recorder so I could record myself, play it back and critic myself. It made me pretty good, especially my singing ability.

At the same time cars and girls became a big topic with all the Bogardus St. Crew, me included. Unlike my friends, however I carried a big stigma. After years of being called crippled boy, possessing a withered leg, a noticeable limp and the inability to perform activities in a natural way, I felt inferior when it came to impressing girls. I didn't ever wear shorts because I was ashamed of the differences in my leg sizes. One leg is over developed from extreme use and the other one the size of a toothpick from the muscles dying, an effect of Polio. Even to this day, the thought of wearing shorts in public scares the hell out of me. Why? Because even in today's society you feel people's eyes watching you just because you limp and I just want to fit in without too much attention paid to my affliction. Besides that, it is one thing that is embarrassing to me no matter what my friends may say to try and convince me that it's ok. I guess some old emotional scars don't ever completely heal.

School dances and party's with dancing were not fun for me. I couldn't hold a girl and use my hand to stabilize my weak leg at the same time, so I thought of myself as an outsider. The few times I tried to dance girls would laugh at me, so I just stopped trying. I felt like an outcast and a failure with women. I buried myself into being a student trainer, played my guitar, and singing. At one point in time I wrote the following song about not being able to dance.

Summer 1962
Following surgery on my unaffected left
leg to slow growth to equalize leg length.

I learned to play the guitar cause I can't dance.
I learned to play the guitar cause I knew there wasn't a chance
That I could dance and stand real tall
And not end up taking a fall
I learned to play the guitar cause I can't dance.
I learned to sing because I don't play so well
I learned to sing cause I don't play the guitar so swell
I thought if I could carry a tune the girls would gather round soon
And hopefully it won't be important to dance.

From the time I was halfway through high school, I became very determined to prove my abilities to everyone, and I must admit it came back later in life to both benefit and haunt me.

During my junior year I was becoming very dependable as a student trainer and I was one of the top dogs in the choir along with a good friend of mine by the name of David Grandi. Dave had the most beautiful and powerful bass voice and played a wonderful piano. I use to go to his house and we would sing and I'd listen to him play. One of the piano pieces he mastered was "Clair De Lune". To this day it is my favorite piece of music and when I die that is the music I want played at my funeral. It starts off soft like we all do as babies; it then becomes fragment like our lives do as we are pulled in many directions. Finally, the music becomes soft, strong and steady much like people do later in life when the beat their challenges. Because of the talent Dave and I had, we could get away with murder in choir rehearsals. Dave was always running off with a girl, and I was always trying to figure out how to impress one. I wasn't wise enough yet to realize that personality is the most important thing and I was always trying to prove myself in the Macho world. Our choir would win competition after competition but no matter what, they would not put me in any stage productions because of my visible disability that the director's would say "would detract from the show".

With the musical production avenue closed to me, I focused on my efforts as a student athletic trainer and working with all the sports teams. At the same time I continued to keep the score book for Mr. Duarte's Varsity Basketball Team. At this point in time, I was approaching my senior year and I was an average student at best. I had no clue where my future was going, but it did not look promising. I wasn't going to go straight to a four year college, I had no major and I still couldn't impress the girls. I felt stupid, worthless and lonely.

As my senior year was passing, I learned more and more about sports injuries while working the football, basketball and baseball seasons. My biggest hurdle that year was trying to overcome the Polio Stigma I grew up with, because it truly affected my relationships with girls. I felt inferior to other guys, I wasn't successful in sports, I couldn't dance and I didn't get a chance to prove myself in school shows. I was truly depressed and wondering why I was still on Earth.

I wrote a poem that year that sums up how I felt.

The man who never smiles is always restless
He laughs and jokes but never shows a smile.
And when he jokes he makes you feel he's happy
When really he's unhappy all the while.
If only things would happen that would change him
To change his mouth from frown to smile above
For it's been said and I believe been proven
That a smile is a common sign of love.

I was looking for a direction for my live, but more than that, I wanted to feel loved and needed.

At the end of my senior year Mr. Duarte came up to me and said "Chip have you ever thought of a future as a Professional Athletic Trainer?" I said "no, but is it possible for me?" He said "let me make a phone call and I'll get back to you". A couple of weeks later he calls me in to his office and said "I've talked with Bill Chambers at Fullerton Community College and he's willing to interview you for the one freshman position that he offers each year". I was excited with the news, thanked Mr. Bailey multiple times and went home to tell my parents.

A week or two later I was interviewed by Mr. Chambers at Fullerton along with a few other potential student trainers. He was only going to pick one person, and I wondered, what kind of chance I had competing against all these "able body" interviewees. Well to my surprise he picked me. I was sure Mr. Duarte must have influenced the decision somehow, and I know I was blessed when Bailey Duarte took me under my wing. Without his direction I probably would have continued to swing on those gymnastic rings all through high school and all that would have happened for me is my arms would have gotten longer.

So off to college I was going. I now had a career in mind, one no disabled person had yet been successful at, but I was going to change that. The only drawback was I still couldn't impress the girls, and I still hadn't figured out how.

CHAPTER
5

As the fall of 1967 approached, I was preparing to attend Fullerton Junior College (FJC). It was a 15 mile drive from our house, but I was ready. I was excited about working for Bill Chambers and I was equipped with a brand new 1967 Ford Mustang to get there.

The football season was starting 2 weeks before school and those first 14 days we had practice twice a day. With all 150 players having to have their ankles either taped or wrapped, it meant early mornings and late evenings for the training staff. We would get to the training room at 4:30 a.m. to prepare for the first practice. With a staff of only Bill, a sophomore student and me, there was a lot of work to do in preparation for the day ahead. One of the things I had to do was cut 125 oranges into quarters for each daily practice. On one of those early mornings because I was still half asleep, as I was cutting the oranges, I cut deep into the tip of my right ring finger because I had left it exposed to the blade under an orange I was slicing. It was bleeding like crazy. I went to the training room first aid station, found some magical dressing to stop the bleeding and back to slicing I went. You can be sure from that time on I was always aware of the position of my fingers while cutting anything.

That first year at Fullerton was exciting. Our team, coached by Hal Sherbeck, was continuing a winning streak that ran over 40 in a row.

I was learning in the classroom and I was truly being educated by Bill Chambers. A couple of weeks into the semester the other student trainer quit leaving just two of us to take care of the team. It was tough with just Bill and I, but the knowledge I gained and the bond the two of us built has lasted until today.

One other fact was changing too, I was starting to recognize that girls liked me for who I was, and it didn't matter who I wasn't. The first girl that helped me realize that was named Dana. For some reason she had a way of making me not feel ashamed of my abnormalities, but had me concentrate on my attributes. She also was the first woman that actually caressed my body, including my right leg, and made me feel my body was acceptable to women who cared about me. As I became aware of that fact, it opened up a new world for me. It gave me confidence that over the years led to many wonderful, exciting and loving experiences with women.

Soon the football season ended and the team went undefeated. Other sports were in full swing and either Bill or I worked them all. It truly gave me great knowledge in what I was doing and it built confidence in Bill that not only was I getting good at the trade, I was dedicated to it.

As the first year grew to a close, I was doing fine in my classes, great in the training room, I had a love life, and I felt I fit in. What could possibly happen that would be a deterrent in my life.

Summer 1968 started off as a typical summer for me, but then I had heard that Coach Sherbeck was getting summer jobs for the players that may need work at Disneyland. I went to coach and ask him if he could get me a job as well and he said he would submit my name. The thought of working at Disneyland, a place I visited many times as a child, was exciting to me. A couple days later Coach Sherbeck called me in to his office, and I was excited about the potential job as I walked in and sat down. As soon as I sat down I knew something was up because Coach Sherbeck would always get big sad puppy eyes when something wasn't right. It was a face I had seen many times whenever he learned about losing a football player for the season due to injury. Anyway from behind his desk he looked up at me and said, they're not going to hire you. I was told you are an insurance risk and more importantly you would be a negative connotation to a positive world. I didn't know how to react; I thanked coach for trying to get me a job and walked out with those words "negative connotation in a positive world" stuck in my head. After all the efforts I had made to try and overcome the psychological stigma of my disability, I was shot down without a chance to even prove myself.

I went home and told my parents about my disappointment, and they too were shocked. Now let me tell you this, the Marchbank family has been in California since the mid 1800's, so there are some long term roots in the area. When my aunt heard about what happened, she called one of her friends that she sold all the corn she grew to and he then sold the corn in his wife's restaurant. I was told my aunt said "Hey Wally, my nephew needs a job, give him one". Right after that I get a call from Knott's Berry Farm asking me if I wanted a job for the summer.

Knott's was a wonderful place to work, and I worked there the year before and the year after they put up the first fence. My job was as a popcorn vendor in a popcorn stand. It was no ordinary stand though; it was the stand that Walter and Misses Knott would stop by every night to pick up a bag of popcorn as they walked the park. Along with enjoying working there, my math skills improved.

At the end of the summer of 68 once again Bill, myself and a new freshman student trainer were back hard at work in the training room. It was a relief to have an additional person working with us. He was new, so he got to slice the oranges every morning.

Our football team was on a 46 game winning streak and we were loaded with talent again. Our quarterback was Jim Fassell from Anaheim High School, and he had a golden arm. Many of you probably remember Jim from his coaching days after he finished playing. His top coaching achievement happened in 2001 when he took his NFL New York Giants Team to the super bowl. That was 33 years after he played at Fullerton and on that Giants Team

Bus heading to the Super Bowl, sitting right next to Jim was Coach Sherbeck. That is the kind of respect that Hal had earned and deserved from all associated with him as a coach, friend and mentor.

Anyway, during that 1968 season, we were once again undefeated going into the semifinal game for the state championship. We had a 57 game winning streak that tied Coach Sherbeck with University of Oklahoma head coach Bud Wilkerson for the longest winning streak in college football history. We went down to San Diego to play San Diego City College at Balboa Stadium to see who would advance to the finals. It was an extremely physical game and at the end we lost 7-0. After the game as the team filed into the locker room, I remember it left only Coach Sherbeck and I standing outside. He probably doesn't remember the moment, but I looked over at him and he looked back he then lowered his head deep in thought. I knew his frustration had nothing to do with the snapping of the winning streak or even the loss. This humble man only was thinking of the disappointment of his players and the fact that this team was now gone forever.

Whether it is true or not, I like to believe I was part of the team coach was going to miss, because he always treated me as an equal to his players and I was going to be transferring as well as the other sophomores. As 1969 approached, I was off to Long Beach State University where my future career would soon be set in stone.

CHAPTER
6

During my stay at Fullerton College Bill Chambers taught me not only about athletic training, but about structure and discipline when working with athletes. As I began my tenure at Long Beach State with Tom Oxley, I was going to learn about making decisions and being flexible. These two men were as far apart in the way they ran their programs as conservatives and liberals are in finding common ground. However, I liked the idea of leading, so it was a perfect place for me. When I started at Long Beach there was Tom, myself a head assistant named Vic and Paul another new young guy like me. The interesting thing about this new training experience was that we got paid! Real money! It wasn't a lot of money as I recall but it was something. So, every day I would go to class and whenever possible I was working in the training room treating the injured athletes.

That first football season was a real experience. We had a new coach Jim Stangeland who had come from USC and he brought with him a 6' 1', 210 lb. sculptured running back that ran a 9.5 100yds. and his name was Leon Burns. He was a star to be. For the next two seasons Leon would run over, around or through every player that got in his way and he made a winner out of the 49ers.

That first season however started off rough and memorable for all of us. Coach Stangeland decided to take the team for the first 2 weeks of practice to Terminal Island Navy Base. We didn't have two a day practices there, we had four a day practices. Early morning running followed by a full practice then a lunch break to eat in the Mess Hall then back for another full practice followed by an evening run. Many a player went AWOL never to be seen again. The sleeping arrangements were less than desirable as well, three high bunk beds in old shower stalls in a locker room. Yes, it was quite the luxury.

Being there for those two weeks did mesh the players, coaches and trainers into a unified team. I can't remember what our record was that year, but I do know we won more than we lost.

When the football season was over, basketball began with the team being coached by a new energetic coach named Jerry Tarkanian. He had molded his team with a truly unique group of players, including an incoming super star freshman named Ed Ratliff. In those days, freshmen couldn't play on the varsity team, so we had a freshmen team. Guess who ended up the trainer for that team! Yes, it was yours truly. We would travel around California beating up on other college teams and grooming Ed for things to come, and boy did he prove himself.

As for me, when I originally transferred to Long Beach, my goal was to be a physical therapy major. It was a very good way to insure you could get a job in sports medicine. So, in the spring semester I applied for the program. There was a one year wait before you were considered to get in, so that year I finished the prerequisites required for the major. At the same time, I continued to work in the training room, honing my skills.

That year both our football and basketball teams went on to be very successful. It was that year I started working with the track team and I met a remarkable man named Jack Rose, he was the head coach for track at the college. The passion that man had for the sport was unmatched by any coach I have ever met, before or after that time. He had a very feisty assistant coach named Ted Banks who was not only very knowledgeable about the running events; he was the chief recruiter for the team. Later on in his career, Ted went on to coach at UTEP where he won a number of national track team championships. During that 1971 track season at Long Beach State, I have one vivid memory. We were hosting a home track meet against USC and over in the parking lot was an old car with the trunk open. Behind the car were a number of players gathered, so I walked over to see what was going on. As I got close, I saw the exchange of money between the athletes and two guys by the open trunk. As I looked in the trunk, I saw these bright orange boxes with big white swoosh on them. Yes, it was the early beginnings of Nike, when they would sell out of the trunk of a car.

When the spring semester ended it was time for me to be interviewed for entrance into the Long Beach State Physical Therapy Program and I went in for my interview confident about my chances. The program was impacted, but hey, I had quite a bit of experience and knowledge from my athletic training duties, so I thought I was ready.

While sitting in the interview, I was dealt another blow. The director of the program said to me, "we are concerned about your ability to transfer patience to wheelchairs because of your disability. Before we consider you for the program, get a job in a physical therapy department somewhere and prove you can handle the work". I walked out of the interview shocked: I was being forced to prove myself once again!

That summer in 1971, I was able to get a job as a physical therapy assistant at a Whittier Hospital. My job was to perform the exact duties that were being questioned by the Long Beach State Program Director. During that time, I was able to carry out the exact the duties that were being questioned. I do remember one mishap however. One day, I took a little old granny out of her bed and put her in a wheelchair and began to push her towards the physical therapy department. We got about 3 feet away from the bed and were pulled back, like a bungee cord was attached to the chair. I pushed again, and had the same result. I then looked down to see that I had forgotten to remove her catheter bag from the bed! I looked at her to apologize and saw a little smile on her face. I made sure that never happen again.

At the end of the summer, I was armed with a letter from the chief physical therapist of the hospital stating I was more than capable to participate in the physical therapy program. I walked into the director's office, gave him the letter and waited patiently while he read it. After he finished reading he looked up and said, "This is impressive, but we have so many normal students to choose from, we are not going to accept a disabled individual into the program". I was crushed. Once again I was being judged without a chance to prove myself. What was I going to do now for a major?

As the fall of 1971 approached we had a new superstar running back join our football team named Terry Metcalf. He was the greatest all around athlete I had ever seen. Terry was fast, agile, could long jump 25 feet and triple jump 56 feet. As a running back he was so elusive, it was like he was in 2 places at once. It was setting up to be a great season.

Mean while I was searching for a major. My boss Tom and I discussed it and decided I should apply to become a physical education major, so I applied. Once again however my disability was called into question. You see, as a Long Beach State P. E. Major, you must select and participate in various coaching classes. Unfortunately, you were required to take either a wrestling or a gymnastics class and neither of those instructors wanted me in the program.

Great, what avenue was available to me now? In stepped the assistant athletic director for the university, Bob Westhoff, and he went to bat for me in a closed door meeting with all the physical education instructors. An hour or so later he came in to the training room where I was working, and he said "Chip you're in". I found out later that it truly was a struggle for him to convince them to accept me, but he did it.

At last, I had a major and I was on the path to graduation. I still would have to prove myself to all the teachers, but at least I had the chance.

As my junior year at Long Beach began the college football program once again had a dominating running game with the elusive Terry Metcalf leading the way. By season's end the team was on the way to a bowl game, I was finally in classes that were going to lead to graduation and my biggest task was going to be to impress the instructor of a required gymnastics class. That specific professor was one of the two individuals that happened to be dead set against letting me into the physical education program. During the first day of his class he took me aside and told me that he would not adapt the curriculum at all for me, and I would be lucky to pass the class. Wow, do you think that put pressure on me? Yes, with that said, it certainly was going to make it a tough semester for me.

Up until now in my story, I have not talked about me participating in weekend sports with my neighborhood friends. For many years we played baseball, basketball and football games on Sunday afternoons. During the fall of my junior year at Long Beach, while hopping around in a Sunday pick-up football game, another player fell on my right foot causing a major fracture. I hopped off to the hospital on my strong leg. I ended up in a cast for months, until I could finally tolerate weight on my foot again. As long as I had a cast on, I could walk on the foot for short distances, but I used crutches most of the time. I bring this up for two reasons; First, I still had to participate in the gymnastics class and second, because of the fact that our 49ers football team made a bowl game, I was chosen to accompany our basketball team during a mid-west swing. I was going with Tark, Ed Ratliff and the rest of the team to Chicago and Milwaukee, I was on crutches, in a cast and there was snow and ice on the ground.

Now I must tell you, as talented as that basketball team happened to be that year, compassion was not in their make-up. I had to carry and handle my own luggage, including my training medical bag. Imagine, walking in the snow with your clothes bag in one hand and a medical bag in the other, while balancing on crutches and wearing a cast. Hey, I'm no superstar player but that was a pretty impressive accomplishment. Anyway, on that trip we played three games with the final stop being a game against Marquette University and their coach Al McGuire.

The night of the Marquette Game, that was played in the Milwaukee Arena, during the pre-game, an event happened that burnt an everlasting memory in Jerry Tarkanian's mind. Just before the game started and after our team's starting line-up was announced, all the lights went out and these mind rattling tom toms started playing. A spot light came on and highlighted each of Marquette's starters as they came out on the court, and trust me, it was very intimidating. We ended up losing the game in a close contest, but later on in his career, Tark developed and used that same intimidation technique in the Shark Tank during his time at UNLV.

Upon our return from that mid-west trip, where we won 2 out of 3 games, we found out the football team had won the bowl game. More important to me however, was that after a week away from school and me still being in a cast, I had to return and perform the gymnastics curriculum.

On my first day back in class, the instructor was making all the members do pull-ups and bar dips. I couldn't believe it, that's right up my alley. When it was my turn to demonstrate my abilities, I led the entire class when I performed 23 full pull-ups and 38 full bar dips. From that day on the instructor looked at me in a more positive light. In every aspect of the required curriculum for that class, I was able to adapt and adjust my abilities and by the end of the term, I earned the respect of the instructor and a B grade in the class.

By far the most exciting event in Cal. St. Long Beach athletic history had to be March Madness 1971 when we went to the Western Regional Championships and played in the championship game against UCLA. The final game was played at the University of Utah in Salt Lake City, where earlier in the week both our teams won our first round match-ups.

It was an amazing contest with Ed Ratliff and George Trapp on our team leading the scoring that gave us a 10 point lead late game. At that point, with about 5 minutes left in the game, Ratliff fouled out and UCLA started to come back and ultimately tied the game with only seconds left. At that time, Tark called timeout.

Let remind you about my past, remember during my high school days, I kept the scorebook for Lowell, and because of that ability, when the Long Beach State Basketball team traveled; I would keep the book for them. So here we were, late in the game against UCLA having a chance to make it to the Final Four Championships and I was the official scorer. While I was sitting there looking down at the scorebook and I heard a voice ask me "Excuse me, can you please tell me how many timeouts we have left?" I looked up to see John Wooden looking at me. I answered his question and he thanked me; Imagine all that excitement and pressure and he still demonstrated poise and respect.

During that time out Tark told our players to inbound the ball, work it around and then feed it to George Trapp at the corner of the key so he could take the final shot at the buzzer. The teams set up on the court and we in bounded the ball, and started pass the ball around, when all of a sudden, one of our guards dropped into the deep corner with the ball and threw up a brick. Only the UCLA player Sidney Wickes was standing under the basket and he grabbed the air ball. He then tossed it down the court to Henry Bibby on a fast break, who dropped the ball through the basket at the buzzer. The game was over and we lost. There is no doubt it was a huge loss for Long Beach, but I'm sure it was the most devastating loss Tark ever suffered in his illustrious career. After all it was John Wooden and we had him beat.

The spring semester was now upon us and the track and baseball seasons were in full swing and I once again was traveling with the track team. Along with Terry Metcalf, we added a new talent to the team, a crazy pole vaulter named Steve Smith who had no concern for the well being of his body which kept me quit busy taking care of his injuries. Steve was an amazing athlete that could vault over 18 feet, which was extreme high for the time. A year later Steve as a vaulter and Ed Ratliff as a basketball player would make the 1972 USA Olympic Team and they would be off to Munich, where they both would be part of the historic controversy and tragedy.

When I look back at those days it is amazing to me to think of all the things I had been a part of while navigating all the physical, emotional, and social barriers placed in front of me. At that time however, all I concentrated on was perfecting my trade and little did I know, like in the verse of a song, "you ain't seen nothing yet".

CHAPTER
7

As the end of my junior year at Long Beach grew to a close, I received an interesting offer. It seems the Los Angeles Rams Football Team was going to use our Long Beach State Facilities that summer for their preseason practice venue. They wanted to hire an assistant trainer that knew the lay of the land, so they came to me and I was offered the job, of course I took it. Getting paid and getting professional experience was a no brainer.

My work with them actually started that spring at their regular training facility in Long Beach, where we would open up the training room and weight lifting facility for player needing treatments and a place to work out before camp started. The head trainer was a crusty "old school" trainer named George Menifee and Cash Birdwell a funny lighthearted physical therapist/athletic trainer was his fulltime assistant. Both of these men were extremely knowledgeable about sports medicine and applying the trade to professional athletes. Along with them was Bill Hewitt the Rams Equipment Man and me. That group of men was all business when necessary and spirited jokesters when there was time to burn. Working with these guys and the array of professional athletes that came through the doors exposed me to a whole new world in sports, the world where it was a business, not just a competition. Anyhow, working that summer and following fall with the Rams was a pleasure and a tremendous learning experience.

Just because I was working with the Rams didn't mean my classes or work assignments at Long Beach stopped. I finished up my spring classes and my track assignment, which cleared my plate for the summer and working with the 1972 Los Angeles Rams with new owner Carol Rosenbloom and Head Coach Tommy Prothro.

I can best describe working with those particular athletes in 4 words; crazy, talented, egotistical, and prideful. I was now part of the team and one thing was for sure, I was going to take it for what it was, a great opportunity and believe me I was going to enjoy the ride.

The opening that I filled with the Rams gave me true insight to the differences in working in the professional game. Practices were much more condensed on the field and much more expanded in the film room and team meetings. The injuries were just as real, but the pressure was put on the doctors and trainers to expedite recovery time and get the players back on the field. In those The days muscle relaxants, anti-inflammatories, and pain killers were all set out on the counter like candy for the players to help themselves to. Doctors didn't hesitate to inject numbing agents into a player come game time, and the players would inject each other with Vitamin B12 before games. One particular player always was the first one to the Coliseum come game day and he and I would sit and talk. I remember one day while we were talking he ask me what time it was. After I told him, he said to me "Well it's time to psyche up"; he shook the cup in his hand and you could hear the numerous pills rattling around inside it as he headed for the drinking fountain. More than anything however, the one thing all of these players had in common was the pay check. They were willing to take any risk to perform at their best and protect their job.

The quarter back for the team that year was, Roman Gabriel. Not only was he talented, he was tough as they come. One day at practice, he suffered a collapsed lung. He refused to be carried in to the training room on a stretcher and insisted on walking in. Imagine the pain you would suffer with a lung malformed putting internal pressure on other organs, along with the breathing complications it would cause. He was one tough dude and returned to the field within two weeks.

Probably the most notable memory I have about my time with the Rams occurred in a home game against the Minnesota Vikings. Merlin Olsen, a hall of fame 280lb. defensive lineman, had sprained an ankle and was rolling around on the field. I ran out to him and he asked me to help him get up. He grabbed my arm and I pulled as hard as my 170lb disabled body could pull and I got him to his feet. Once he was up, he put his massive hand on top of my head, pushed down and using me and my skull as a crutch to get off the field. As we were both were limping along, I said to myself, "this will never happen again". It was at that point in time when I came up with the idea that when a player is hurt, and if they can be assisted off the field; I will get 2 players of equal or bigger size to assist them off.

The experience I had with the Rams was wonderful and I made some lifetime friends, but I still needed to finish my senior year at Long Beach State and my loyalty was still to them. At one time I was working for the Rams, Long Beach and going to school. It was wonderful, but I have to admit I was glad when the Rams season was over, and life would return to a normal pace; At least for a while.

During the fall semester of 1972 as I said I was working with the LA Rams, working Long Beach State Football, going to school and being from East Whittier commuting became a big issue. Luckily for me, I had an old high school friend whose grandparents owned a beach house in Surfside Beach, a private beach colony that was only 10 minutes from the campus. My friend's family only used the place in the summer, so I was able to rent it during the school year for $100.00 a month, all utilities paid! What a perfect set-up, I was almost done with school, I was working with Long Beach State, the LA Rams and I was living in a three story beach front house. I won't go into the craziness that happened at the beach house, but it did involve Ed Ratliff and Steve Smith from time to time.

There is one account I would like to share with you concerning my time in the beach house and it involved my father. The house I lived in didn't have a phone, and of course there were no cell phone back then. The bedrooms of the house were on the third floor and one night at about 2:00am I was woken by the sound of pebbles hitting my bedroom window. I got up, looked out the windowpane to see my father standing in the street. When he saw me, he waved and started to walk away to leave. I hurried down stairs, stopped him and ask what the matter was. He told me he had a terrible nightmare and he was worried about me, so he got in his truck drove one hour just to see me through the window and make sure I was alright. I always knew my father loved me, but at that moment I realized how much.

Life was good and I was close to graduating with a degree in Physical Education; Emphasis in Sports Medicine. It was something most people never thought was in the cards for a disabled person, yet alone a Polio Survivor. I was now thinking in my mind, what now? Where do I go from here? I had no offers for work after the spring, except for perhaps a low paying job with the Rams and I was concerned. Little did I know that before the spring semester would start, that there would be a major change at Long Beach State that would mean for me, a future in Sports Medicine that few people could ever imagine.

In late December the word was spreading in the athletic department that Tom Oxley, the man that had taken a chance and hired me 3 ½ years earlier was leaving to become head trainer at Northwestern University. That college is in a northern suburb of Chicago and is part of the Big Ten Conference. It is where Tom had worked before coming to Long Beach and the place he hoped to return to some day. What it did at Long Beach was make the second year fulltime assistant trainer Dan Bailey the new head trainer and it elevated me to assistant trainer for the spring with a pay increase. It was however a temporary assignment.

As usual, I worked and traveled with the basketball, track and baseball teams. The basketball team lead by Eddie returned to the regional finals held in Provo Utah where once again we were defeated. The track team, lead by Steve Smith and Terry Metcalf, won the conference championships held at San Jose State. I was also finishing my final classes in the physical education department to complete my bachelors' degree. It seemed like that final semester flew by and before I knew it I was down to my final days at the university.

During that time frame I got a phone call from Tom Oxley. He asked me if I would be interested in the fulltime assistant trainer's job at Northwestern. He went on to say I would have to fly back for an interview within a few days, which I was more than willing to do. So the next thing I know I'm on a plane bound for Chicago to interview with Tom, the athletic director and the head football coach. During the interview I found out that the training staff for Northwestern University was also the training staff for the old "College All-Star Game". It was a football game that was played every summer and pitted the top NFL Draft Picks from that year against the current Super Bowl Champions. Anyway, after the interview I spent the evening with Tom and his wife and the next day boarded a plane back to Los Angeles. Soon after I got home, I had a phone message, asking me to please call Tom. When I returned the call he told me I had gotten the job and as soon as my classes were finished I was to report for work at NU.

So, as the semester came to a close I was preparing for the move. I had never lived in the mid-west, so I had to prepare for both the climate and social changes. Because of the fact that I had to report to Northwestern as soon as I could, I had to skip my graduation ceremonies, but I had made it, my classes were complete and I was a college graduate. Uncertain of what God had in mind for me, I was about to leave home, Long Beach State, and California all for an unknown future, but boy did it work out.

CHAPTER
8

As I packed up my new 1973 Ford Pinto with everything I was taking with me, thoughts of a recent plane trip I had taken to Chicago to establish a place to reside while I was working at Northwestern crossed my mind. A number of people advised me to move to the city of Arlington Heights, a city that was about 20 miles northwest of the university campus. The reason I picked that spot was very simple. It is the city where the United Airlines Stewardess School is, and I thought I would be constantly surrounded by beautiful woman. Anyway, it was now time to make the move and I was packing my little car with what I thought I needed; my clothes, guitar, stereo system and a small television. I was now leaving Southern California for a place where I knew the total of one person, Tom Oxley.

Once underway, I remember driving over the California/Arizona border and looking back over my shoulder wondering, will I ever move back to SoCal? It was the only place I'd ever called home, it was familiar and it was growing smaller in my rear view mirror. To me, it was intimidating and exciting at the same time. I was driving away from what I knew and heading into an unknown future; carrying with me strong sports medicine experience, but also carrying the burden of knowing I would have to prove myself once again.

Once I arrived at my new apartment, it only took minutes to unpack; after all I only had those few items. I shopped around locally and bought a bed, some wood planking and cinder blocks. I now had a place to lie down and a homemade shelf to put my stereo and television on. For my needs, the place was now complete and I walked out heading off to the university to check in. As I walked to my car, I was looking around for stewardesses, but there were none in sight and that was a sign of things to come.

It was a beautiful early summer day when I was making my first trip from Arlington Heights to the university in the town of Evanston. It is the neighboring college town that is just north of Chicago, and it took me about 20 minutes to drive there from my apartment. Once I got to the stadium where the sports medicine facility was, I parked my car and headed inside. Tom Oxley was already there doing paperwork of some sort. When he saw me he got a big smile on his face and he came over to greet me. As I looked around the room it was eye catching, because everything was painted either Royal Purple or Bright White, the official school colors. Tom had me sit down and we began to talk about the arrival of the College All-Star Team. The players and coaches were going to be arriving in a couple days and would be staying in a local posh hotel where we were also given rooms to be with the team. The head coach of the team was chosen because of his schools success the year prior, and our coach was going to be John McKay from USC. He was bringing along with him his coaching staff that included future NFL Head Coaches John Robinson and Marv Levy. Among the players that were coming were Burt Jones, Ray Guy John Matuszac, Sam Cunningham, John Hanna, Darryl Stingily, and one of my Long Beach State college associates, Terry Metcalf. Most of the players on the team went on to have long illustrious careers in the NFL. One major exception was wide receiver Darryl Stingily, because two or three years into his New England Patriots career, while running a crossing pattern in a game against the Oakland Raiders, he received a vicious and malicious blow to the head from defensive back Jack

Tadem that instantly turned Darryl into quadriplegic, thus ending his career and putting him into a wheelchair for life. Some years earlier I had established a relationship with Darryl because during his rookie year in the NFL, he got his knee blown out in a game and because he was from Chicago, he chose to do his rehabilitation with Tom and I at Northwestern during his off season. Darrel and I had many conversations during that time about disabilities and their long term effects. It seems eerie in retrospect.

I need to stop here for a minute and ask you a question. Do you think it is more devastating to have a crippling disease or injury as a young child and never having a chance to test your true limits? Or, do you think it is worse to be traumatized somehow later in life and have your proven abilities taken away? Most of the people I ask this question give me the answer, later in life. Why? Because that is a fear that every person faces; losing what they have. In reality however, it is the opposite. Remember, most adults becoming victims are already established in mainstream society, and if this book delivers any message at all, I hope it opens your eyes to the ignorance and cruelty of uninformed children. Please teach your family to demonstrate compassion and inclusion of disabled kids. Don't make the physically and mentally challenged young ones feel like outcasts in the world. It seems the only ones from the group that make it, are the ones that learn to hide their pain.

Sorry, I'll get off my soap box and get back to my story.

So, the 1973 All-Stars where arriving to practice and prepare to play in a game against the undefeated Super Bowl Champion Miami Dolphins. The game was going to be played at a sold out Soldier Field, it was going to be nationally broadcast on ABC and we had three weeks to get ready.

John McKay proved to be a remarkable man. He was extremely intelligent, he was funny, cool under pressure and he and Tom Oxley were going to becoming best of friends, and it was a friendship that would totally affect my future.

When the all-star camp began it was amazing to be flooded with all the press, television media, NFL Official Representatives, NFL Team Representatives, celebrities, advertising agencies, and the general public. Everywhere you would turn, someone was interviewing a player, trying to get a new NFL player as a client or someone trying to get one of the player's autographs.

Every head coach of past all star teams would hold practices twice a day, but John McKay only wanted to practice once a day and spend more time in film studies. It would prove to be a great decision. All these future NFL Stars bought into John's philosophy and put in a major effort to succeed. As the days went by, two players from USC, running back Sam Cunningham, tight end Charlie Young and I became friends. Maybe it was because the three of us were from Southern California or maybe it was because I had a car. No matter what the reason, we hung out at local night spots together. We would go to clubs where people wouldn't recognize who they where and we could enjoy ourselves. I remember at one of the clubs they served something none of us had ever heard of, "French Fried Mushrooms", and instead of dipping them in catsup, you smothered them with mustard. They actually tasted pretty good.

As the game approached the seriousness and tension ratcheted up. ABC Television Producers and the game announcers, Howard Cosell & Bud Wilkerson started coming around. This was the most star studded and exceptional events I ever was associated with, and it truly was a three ring circus.

The evening of the game, massive Soldier Field on the south side of Chicago was overflowing with 100,000 plus people as we took the field. Included in that crowd were my mom, dad, aunt, and uncle who I had gotten tickets for. It was the first time in my entire career as a trainer that my father had come to a game I was working. It was a turning point in his and my relationship, because as much as he loved me, he had no interest in sports. Imagine, he could have had L. A. Ram Tickets, Western Regional Basketball Championship Tickets and array of other special sporting event tickets and he didn't care. I was just happy he finally had come to see me work after all those years.

That event changed my father. After that night, he started flying back to some Northwestern Games and he became a true sports fan, especially if I was involved with the event.

The All Star Game was very exciting that Saturday night in Chicago, in fact, the all-stars took the lead twice that evening but the NFL was not going to have these rookies, coached by a college coach, beat the undefeated Super Bowl Champs. Two times after we scored touchdowns, and well after the play was over, the officials pulled out flags and called the plays back. At one point during the game, which was interrupted by a big rain storm, one of our players was hurt and I was working on him at the sidelines. All my friends in Whittier had gathered together to watch the game and they saw me treating the injury as the camera crew zoomed in tight. After the game that we lost 14-3, John McKay gave a heartfelt thank you and good bye to all of players, coaches and trainers as we all packed up to head our separate ways. Later, when I got home that night, I must have had 20 phone messages from friends excited about seeing me on television that evening. For one brief moment, I felt some satisfaction knowing that I had proven myself in the eyes of my friends, but that feeling quickly went away because I knew they all loved me no matter what, and I wanted bigger results.

As the summer of 1973 was coming to an end, it was time for the Northwestern Wildcat Football Team to take to the practice field. For a number of years the team had struggled to win because the academic standards at NU were so high. Where other Big Ten Universities could get incoming freshman eligible, we couldn't. I'm not saying we weren't talented, but with the rigid restriction we had, it defiantly limited the depth we could have at every position. None the less practice was getting underway and the season was going to be interesting.

If there ever was a place in my story to spend a little time highlighting a team's season it is here, the football season at old NU.

The first thing I must mention is that not one Big Ten Football School is frugal, including Northwestern. For every game, home and away, our team stayed in a hotel the night before. First run movies were brought in for the team to watch the evening before the game. Catered dinners and embellished evening sandwich trays were abundant sparing no expense. The next morning on game day, Tom and I had taping tables set up in the corner of the dining room, and after the players had eaten breakfast, we would start taping their ankles, knees, wrists, thumbs and whatever else needed to be protected prior to heading to the stadium. Once at the stadium, we would finish any additional taping prior to taking the field for warm-ups. This was a standard procedure at all games away or home.

The first memory I have of being on the field of an NU Game was against University of Pittsburg. They had a freshman running back that wasn't even listed on their official roster who ran for five touchdowns against us. We lost a close game, and it was embarrassing. After the game I learned the player's name, it was Tony Dorsett. Tony went on to become a NFL Hall of Fame Running Back who played for the Dallas Cowboys.

The next big game I remember was at Notre Dame and their legendary coach Ara Parsegian. That game was a blow out and we got killed. The memories from that encounter are interesting because after the game the Notre Dame Players came over and started harassing us saying "you suck" and something about our mothers. I remember one of our offensive linemen turning to their players and saying "Hey, you may have beaten us today, but you'll all work for us tomorrow". I must tell you Northwestern University definitely puts out the heads of industry.

Our next stop was at the University of Wisconsin. This was an exciting game that we won. This school is known for their per-game tailgate parties and the smells from the bratwurst cooking as our bus approached the stadium was fantastic. Before the game, as we were walking back to the locker room from warming up on the field, I noticed cyclone fencing suspended over the tunnel to the locker room. I ask Tom what that was there for. He said the fans liked to throw things down at the visiting team and it was protection. As we re-emerged from the locker room to play the game and just before we exited the tunnel, Tom grabbed me by the shoulder and pulled me back. As I watched our team start to funnel out of the tunnel on to the field, I saw a cascade of beer being poured through the cyclone fencing totally dousing our team. After the last drop was poured Tom said; "ok now we go out". It was an amazing experience and made for a lasting memory.

When we went to Ohio State, it was their homecoming game and they had their largest crowd in history to that point. 85,000 plus Buckeye fans watched a Woody Hayes lead team crush us 60-0. It was a disaster because we had high hopes of playing a great game, but we were hit early in the game with a number of injuries to key players dashing any hopes of competing. To this day I have no idea why Woody poured it on us so late in the game when we were so drastically out manned.

Early on a winter Sunday morning the day after one of our home games, I was asleep when my phone rang and woke me up. I picked up the phone to hear a voice saying "Chip its Sam, we're in town to play the Bears and I left tickets for you at Will Call." Now, I truly appreciated the fact that I was offered free tickets to a Patriots/Bears Game, but while lying in bed I reached over, opened the drapes to see snow falling. I then put the phone back to my ear and said "thanks Sam but I don't think I'll make it". Let me tell you, if I would have had the opportunity to meet him somewhere and sit and talk, nothing would have stopped me, but to go sit in a stadium and to watch him or any of my friends perform in an event has never interested me. What truly matters to me, is the personal relationships I have built with them as together we share our triumphs and mutually supporting each other through times of sorrow.

There is one more game I would like to mention. It was a game we won at home and I don't remember the team, but the memory of the situation is perfectly clear. In those days all NU games were broadcast locally in Chicago and Brent Musburger, who went on to a big career, was the local TV announcer. At one point in the game one of our players got hurt on the field and I ran out to treat him. When I got out to him he was grabbing his stomach and screaming in pain. I asked him where does it hurt, something all trainers are taught to ask, but all he did is keep screaming. As I tried to get him to calm down, he wouldn't listen so I started to feel around on his stomach. At that point in time he finally came to his senses and said "it's my ankle". Boy did I look like an idiot on television. Hey Brent, if you happen to read this, that's exactly what happened that cool fall day at good ole Dyche Stadium.

The football season was now coming to an end and we went 4-6 that season. Even thought it was exciting and I learned a lot throughout that period, basketball season was upon us and I was going to be traveling with our new head coach. This was a man who was known to be one of the biggest characters in all of coaching, his name is Tex Winter, and boy was the hype correct!

Long before Phil Jackson hired Tex Winter to bring his famous "Triangle Offense" to the Chicago Bulls and Los Angeles Lakers, Tex was the head coach at Northwestern University.

The first year he coached at NU was 1973, the year I was a trainer there. Tex was an extremely intelligent man, but he was even more of a character. With his heavy southern accent he was always quick with a quip and with his extremely short temper, he was also quick to react.

Following below are two examples I submit as evidence;

The basketball staff, including the trainers, would often go to lunch at least once a week before practice. One day as we were sitting in a restaurant and the waitress was taking our orders, it got to Tex. After he told her what he wanted to eat, she asked him what he would like to drink. He looked at her, picked up his glass of water, stared through the side of the glass and said "I think I'll drink this here water, I don't care if the fish mate in it". That's an example of his southern wit.

One time, we went on a road trip to play in a basketball tournament at Marshall University. It was a fund raising event to help support their football program that a couple of years earlier was devastated when the entire team was killed in a plane crash. By the way, the airliner crashed while trying to land at the same airport that we were now landing.

Marshall University is in Huntington West Virginia, and as I recall, that airport was quite unique, Gate 1 & Gate 2. When our luggage arrived, an attendant announced "Your luggage is here" and someone threw it through a pair of swinging doors and it slid about 20 feet across the floor. Anyway, when we arrived at the gymnasium at Marshall we found that it was so old and small; the only way to fit the team benches in was to put them next to the basket on the end line on opposite ends of the court. During one of our games Tex, was getting frustrated with the officials, and at one point in the game a ball rolled over the end line and ended up at Tex's feet. The ball had bounced off of one of the opposing teams players and the possession should have gone to us, but the official signaled that it go to the other team. As the referee stood frozen like a statue pointing in the opposite direction, Tex took the ball and with vigor, ricocheted off the side of the referees head knocking him off his feet. When the official stood back up, he looked over at Tex to hear him say "Sorry the ball slipped". That's Tex Winter; he is feisty, funny, full of life, and that was one of many adventures I had with the man that year.

Spring had arrived and I had made it first my first real winter, snow and all. I wasn't particularly impressed with the four seasons, give me the sun and sand anytime.

Baseball and track were underway, and in the training room we were preparing for spring football practice. One morning when I entered the training room, Tom called me over. He told me to sit down because he wanted to talk with me. At that point, he had a very serious look on his face as he began to speak. Tom told me John McKay had been hired by the Tampa Bay Buccaneers of the NFL and he wanted Tom to come as the head trainer. The problem was that there was an existing training staff at Tampa, so Tom had no room to take me with him. Although Tom assured me that when the time was right he would bring me to Tampa, it was quite a blow to me. Not because I couldn't leave with him, but because he was the reason I went to Northwestern in the first place and now I faced being there alone and I certainly didn't like it.

Once I had given it some thought, I made the decision to leave NU and go back home. I contacted Dan Bailey the trainer at Cal State Long Beach and ask him if he knew of any job openings in the area. He told me there was an opening at a local Orange County High School in the City of Westminster. I contacted the head coach at the school, a man named Bill Boswell. We had a nice conversation and quickly it was set. At the end of the summer, I would start with him at Westminster High School as his school's athletic trainer. As spring football at Northwestern was drawing to a close both Tom and I were disappointed in the fact that we were going to have to go our separate ways, but for both of us it was going to work out.

My last day at Northwestern was the day of the spring football game. My father had flown out a couple of days earlier to be there for the game and to accompany me on the drive back to California. Right after the game, Tom and I said our goodbyes and my dad and I got in my car and started driving toward the setting sun, the warmth of the place I had come from and little to my knowledge at the time, an exciting new future.

CHAPTER
9

The trip back from Chicago to Southern California that I shared with my father was a wonderful experience. We talked about many things but the most notable to me was my thanking him and my mom for revolving their lives around mine, making sure I got every chance to succeed in life. You see, my dad was a truly gifted artist and my mother was an extraordinary writer. When I was struck by Polio, many of the dreams they may have had were put on hold to make sure that my father had a job with a guaranteed pay check and medical benefits to maximize what they could provide for me. My mother made sure she was at home to attend to all my needs, including many trips to the doctor's office or hospital. My parents never said one word about what they personally forfeited, but as I grew I recognized the extent of the talents they were willing to give up.

On that return trip while my father and I were either driving, sitting in a restaurant, or in a motel room, our conversations revolved around the mutual love and respect we had for each other. He would remind me of things I had accomplished at some point in my early life that I had totally forgotten about, but to him those were moments that had made him proud. I reminded him of things he had done or said that showed his depth of love for me, and I reminded him of the morals he instilled in me that molded me into a man.

As we were approaching the California border, I recognized the same landmarks I was looking at in my rear view mirror just one year earlier. They seemed different to me now though, I had grown more experienced and mature as a person and as for my father; he had developed pride and a new found interest in what I did for a living. Yes, things were certainly different as we approached home, and I wondered what was waiting for me on the other side of that California border.

After a couple of days back in Whittier, I knew I had changed. I no longer would be content living at home with my parents. I needed to move closer to where I was going to be working and I needed to have the freedom that only could be established by not living with your parents.

I talked with a friend of mine named Ed Sawyer about the two of us moving out together. You will read later in the book what happened when I was the best man in his wedding, but at this point all we both wanted was to move out and live by the beach. Perhaps you remember me writing about living at a friend's family beach house in Surfside when I was attending California State Long Beach. Well, I contacted that friend, and he was able to locate a small house down in Surfside Beach for Ed and I to move into.

The interesting thing about that place was it had no bedrooms. It had a loft in the attic and a divider in the kitchen that allowed us to convert the dining room into a bedroom. Ed and I thought the place was great and we decided he would take the dining room and I would take the attic. After all Ed was 6' 5" and there was no way with his large body he would fit or be comfortable in the attic, especially with the exposed roofing nails sticking down through the ceiling.

The rest of the summer was very relaxing. We spent the days on the beach attracting ladies, who then would end up at the wild parties at our beach house at night.

It was a good thing the summer was relaxing, because the football season was about to start and my life was once again going to get crazy. This time however, it would put in motion a commitment that would last for the rest of my working life. So buckle up, I'm telling you the ride was about to get interesting.

As the summer of 1974 came to a close, I began working at Westminster High School with the Lion Football team. When I first stepped into the training room, I was shocked; it was about the size of a walk-in closet, and after seeing how limited space was, it was apparent that I was going to have to be very creative in how I used it. As always, I could count on my father to help me come up with an answer. He and I designed a large table that had multiple taping stations and a large storage cabinet in the base. It was perfect for my needs, and to my knowledge, that table was still in use at Westminster High as late as 2004.

That season was the first time in my training career that I had to work with multiple levels of football teams, a freshman, sophomore, junior varsity and varsity team. It was truly challenging to treat that many athletes, but I have a belief that you have to treat ALL athletes the same. It doesn't matter what level they compete at or what their sport was, I treated them all and was exhausting.

As the pre-season progressed, we would have players hurt ankles, knees, and other body parts, and we did not have any modalities to treat them. I was used to using sophisticated equipment at NU, and all we had at Westminster was a whirlpool and ice. Coach Boswell told me that the local community college had the equipment we needed and if I wanted to send the injured players over to their facility, the college trainer would treat them for me.

Immediately I began to take advantage of that favor and I began sending athletes to Golden West College for treatment. One interesting point was, because of my vast experience, I was asking the college trainer to perform treatment techniques he wasn't familiar with. In fact, I guess it prompted him to realize that the profession was passing him by and I received a phone call from him. He told me that he was going to step down as the trainer, and he felt strongly that I should apply for the job.

Now it has always been my belief that I owe loyalty to the people that are willing to take a chance on me, and with that in mind, I told the trainer thanks but no thanks. A couple of days later, the Westminster Head Football Coach Boswell stormed in to the high school training room and came straight over to me. He took me aside and said to me "are you nuts?" I said what are you talking about? He went on to say that he had heard from the college trainer that I wasn't interested in the job because of loyalty. Coach Boswell then insisted that I apply for the job with the commitment that for that one season, I would work all the Westminster Varsity Football Games for him. So, with that in mind, I reluctantly applied at Golden West College.

I remember interviewing with the college athletic director, a man named Fred Owens. He asked me questions about my experiences at Northwestern University, Long Beach State University and the College All-Stars, but he was most interested about my experience with the Los Angeles Rams. Following a nice conversation with Fred, I left and went back to the high school.

A few days later I got a call asking me to come back and visit with Fred Owens once again. My memory is very clear about that second meeting. He set me down in his office and said to me, "I need to make a decision, and I don't have unanimous support among our coaches on who to hire". He went on to say that some of the Golden West Football Coaches questioned my ability to get injured players off the field. Fred then leaned forward over his desk and said to me; "I told them, Chip has worked for the Rams, he's figured it out." At that moment Fred put out his hand and said to me "welcome aboard".

Once again my futures was changing, and guess what, that was the last time ever in my life I ever had to deal with someone openly doubting my abilities. However, once again, I was going to have to go out and prove myself.

CHAPTER
10

It was an uncanny feeling the first day I stepped into the Golden West College Training Room to work. It was a small facility attached to the equipment room, but what felt different was I was back in a college setting, and I was the boss. There was no one to look to for support or to help me with decision making. Nope, now it was sink or swim on my own. I had prepared for a long time for this and I had confidence in my skills, but proving myself to a group of 100% strangers was going to be a challenge.

The first person I met was the equipment manager, Ernie Moersch. He was a gruff X-Marine who trusted very few people. The storage room for the training supplies was in the back of the equipment room and every time I would pass by Ernie on my way to or from the training storage area, he would give me the once over to make sure I hadn't grabbed a t-shirt, a pair of shorts or a jock. After sensing his discomfort with me, one time as I was passing back by him, I stopped, pulled up my shirt and performed a 360 degree turn showing him I had nothing on me that he should be concerned about. He laughed and from that point on we bonded like a second father and son.

As the players started coming in to get taped and prepare for practice, they were amazed at the speed, accuracy and comfort I would apply their protective tape. Any accomplished trainer can fully tape an ankle with a sophisticated strapping technique in less than 60 seconds. This is a skill that takes time to prefect because each piece of tape is applied with a specific purpose to prevent injury. One thing that happens when you possess superior taping skills is it immediately builds confidence with the athletes, and they share that with their teammates and coaches. This then helps build your reputation as a professional among the various teams.

After the 2 hour taping session was over and all the players were prepared, I went out to football practice. As I was standing there, out of the corner of my eye I saw a man approaching me. This person walked up to me and said, "Hi I wanted to introduce myself, my name is Tom Noon and I know I'm only the cross country/track coach but I wanted to say hi". As I shook his hand, I looked him in the eye and replied, "What do you mean only the cross country coach. I want you to know I treat athletes from all sports exactly the same. With me, it is first come first served, no favoritism". He then looked at me and smiled, and one fact that I am very proud of is that over the years I proved to every coach that particular conviction was always true.

One of the most important relationships a trainer can have is with the local medical community. You need to have a good relationship with the specialists in the area and you need an outstanding team physician and preferably an orthopedic surgeon to serve in that capacity. So, immediately I began my quest to find a quality doctor for Golden West College.

While I was exploring the options we had, I came across the name of a young orthopedic surgeon practicing and living in Huntington Beach by the name of Robert Cassidy and what a beautiful match it was going to become. The first time Robert "Butch" Cassidy and I met was in his modest office. We set and talked at length about our expectations concerning building a sports medicine program at the college. It was like we were twins, we wanted the same things. Treat all our athletes, no matter want kind of insurance they had. The doctor would commit to coming into the training room at least once a week, at a set time for the entire year to see and evaluate all injured athletes. He would work all the football games and whenever possible, I could go and observe the corrective surgeries that our injured players would have, so I could better understand what would be appropriate for each individual's rehabilitation regiment. It was a perfect match and it grew into more than a working relationship, we became best of friends. With that achievement, the medical coverage at the college was developing, but I still had to gain the confidence of the coaches.

Once again I'm going to stop my story for a moment to expound on a very important point I've learned since writing this book. It truly doesn't matter what motivates and drives an individual to succeed, but I hope by unveiling the story about the struggles I went through helps you recognize why throughout my life I was so driven. It is important for my friends that take the time read this to understand that one fact about me. As I said at the beginning of the book, I've never wanted to be better than anyone, I've only wanted to be equal to everyone, and that's the truth. Those many days in my life that I was mocked and made fun of, the times I was told I didn't fit in or couldn't perform the work just added additional height to a barrier that already seemed insurmountable because of having to overcome a disability. So understand, that the fire that one builds inside to be successful, cannot just be turned off because family, friends and acquaintances think you have succeeded. In my case, success has pushed me that much harder, I've always been afraid that if I let up, even for a second, I'll fall behind everyone else. It's kind of a "Keeping up with the Jones" belief. I will tell you that having that kind of dedication to achieve something is very tiring and it can keep you from enjoying your success, or recognizing the beauty of a sunset, or hearing the sounds of a bubbling brook or even appreciating the smell of a beautiful flower. I truly don't recommend that kind of commitment, but it wasn't my choice; It was pushed on me by people that didn't relate to what their decisions were causing to happen to my segment of society. I understand no one purposely put pressure on me to overcome the obstacles that were put in front of me, but that was the outcome and it has become traumatic. Knowing I have alienated people that wanted to be close to me, because they ended up feeling second choice to my drive to becoming successful, has really hurt me.

There is one final thought I would like to share here; I truly fear in my heart and soul, that because of the constant drive I have inside, I will never be able to stop testing the limits of my abilities until the day comes I finally die. Yes people respect me for what I've achieved and I've enjoyed quite a bit of success, but boy what an enormous cost. What is truly sad is, I would love to be able to turn off the force that pushes me just for awhile so I could take time to truly enjoy a moment, any moment.

Now let's return to the summer of 1974. As the first couple of weeks of team practices went by at Golden West, I developed a great relationship with the athletes, but the football coaching staff was a different story. The coaches weren't use to having a professional athletic trainer that had more knowledge than them about injuries and the proper treatment of them and it was going to take time to build that trust.

It has always been a standard practice with football teams at all levels that the trainer briefs the coaching staff first thing every Monday morning following a game about the number and severity of any injuries the players may have sustained in the weekend contest. At first, I would go into the coach's office and explain in technical terms what had happened to each affected player. When I was done explaining the extent of the injuries, they would thank me for telling them and I would leave. A few days after our second game, Ernie, the equipment man, told me that the coaches believed I was talking down to them with all the technical jargon. It was an eye opener to me, I was use to that type of presentation in the other settings I had worked, but I then realized that was among other trainers, not the coaching staff. So the next time I went in on a Monday, I broke my descriptions down into simpler terms. Once again the coaches thanked me and I left. The next thing I know Ernie is back in my office telling me that now the coaching staff thought I was talking down to them like they were children, I thought, I can't win!

I was bewildered and concerned about what I could do to balance my presentation to the coaches. I decided to go and talk with Dr. Cassidy on how to deal with the issue, so I drove over to his office and he and I set down in his office to chat. It was amazing what this highly educated down to earth physician from Georgetown University told me. At first he laughed, then he said; "Chip, you need to think about the issue from their point of view." He said that the most important thing to realize is they don't want to hear what you have to say because it never is good news. Secondly, you can't just be matter of fact about the injuries; these coaches have built strong relationships with these players, and they're like a family. Lastly, you need to show compassion, explain things in the same way you would want to hear them yourself. I stood up thanked Dr. Cassidy and said to him "lesson learned". After that conversation, I never had a communication problem with a coach again.

As my first season at GWC progressed, I was able to generate interest among some of the college students to volunteer to work with me in the training room. The first person to volunteer was an individual named Ron Eagle. He was as dedicated to the profession and to me as any person could possibly be and if I was working an event, he was always by my side. Ron was the first in a string of student trainers that worked with me over the years and many of them went on to have very successful careers as a professional trainer. There were 12 total that I was blessed to have work with me that went on to graduated from a four year university and become a force in the profession. I am not sure how much of an impact I really had on them, but I do know that my training philosophies went with them and were established in their athletic training practices. Over the years most of them have stayed in contact with me, and it makes me very proud to see so many of my former students succeed in a profession where many individuals that attempt to be successful, don't make it.

That first year was full of growing pains for me. Adjusting to a training facility that was very small and restrictive, developing relationships with the various team coaches who all had their own strong beliefs and egos, trying to build a support staff to help in the training room, and the frustrating effort I dealt with trying to get buy in with everyone involved who didn't understand my training concepts.

As that first year ended, the relationship I had with Dr Cassidy was growing stronger and stronger, the rapport with the coaches was slowly beginning to develop and the best thing of all that happened that year was the athletic director, Fred Owens, was proud of his decision to hire me. To him, I had brought skills, knowledge and credibility to the Golden West Sports Medicine Program for the first time, and he liked it.

That spring, I realized I was making inroads within the athletic department, but I also knew if I wanted to truly develop a sports medicine program, I would have to look outside of our department and build relationships with other individuals, departments and administrators. It was going to take some time, but trust me; the effort was going to pay off.

In the summer of 1975 and knowing that if you want to have a program flourish you must have support throughout your organization, so I started visiting the departments that can truly make or break your success.

My first stop was going to be the Golden West College Grounds Department. There I was to encounter a man named Mike Hemphill, and he and I were to become lifelong friends.

The first year I worked at the college I would borrow an electric cart from him to move training supplies to and from athletic fields. When I would go out to get a cart, the two of us would sit and talk about many subjects. From time to time, if he had a medical question about himself or one of his family members I would either answer it or refer him to someone who could. If at any time there was someone he wanted me to treat for an injury, he could consider it done.

At the time, I didn't realize it, but Mike was developing a trust and respect for my medical knowledge, but more important he was building a belief in me as a true friend who cared about him and his convictions. In turn, even though I usually didn't ask, Mike paid attention to my needs and was willing to support me in any way he could to make it easier for this old polio survivor. Mutual caring made our relationship very strong, and it became like we were brothers, a relationship that is just as strong today.

I've always felt Mike did far more to support me and my programs success than I could ever repay him. Over the years he would become very involved in any way he could to insure the training program was successful. He made sure I always had my own electric cart and if there was anything I needed to improve services, and if he had a say in the matter, it was going to happen.

I want you to know one thing more about this very caring man. Although he was extremely supportive of my program, his true concern had always been protecting my physical well being. Thanks in no small part to Mike Hemphill, my program and I flourished.

Other relationships started to develop on campus as well. It seemed the word was out that if someone that worked on campus, or one of their family members, had an orthopedic problem, they were told to check with Chip, he'll know what to do. Not only did individuals on campus start coming in to see me, but top administrators throughout the district would contact me as well with questions. Between Dr. Cassidy, the other medical providers I had built relationships within the community and me, we could insure that anyone asking was going to get the best in medical care.

What was the outcome from all of that? People began to believe in me, the ideas I had and they trusted my program. What was even a crazier result was that within in a few short years I was going to develop an idea that would allow me to ask for the moon and get it.

CHAPTER
11

As the 1975-1976 school year approached I received the most interesting phone call. The head trainer for the Rams was calling me to see if I would be interested in being the trainer for the jockeys at Los Alamitos Race Track. That group of horsemen was looking for someone to work in the "Jockeys Room" race nights and treat their injuries. I said I would be interested if it didn't conflict with my commitment to Golden West and I agreed to meet with the jockey's representative.

It turns out that the quarter horse season didn't conflict with my work schedule at the college so I agreed to do it. You all have heard the saying, "What happens in Vegas stays in Vegas". Well, the jockeys live by that creed in their facility long before it was a popular saying. I witnessed things while working with them that not only were unusual but were amazing as well. The life style they lived and the abuse these men and one lady put themselves through night after night to prepare to race, was truly shocking. Most of them would be up every morning at 4 am riding horses that were training for future competition. After that they would go to the steam room and sit in there for hours to lose weight for that night's races. Every so often they would come out to eat a popsicle and then return inside with the steam where they had board games to play so they could occupy the hours of agony they put themselves through. Once the jockeys came out to get ready for racing, many of the veterans would swallow stimulants to get their energy levels up to compete. Once the nights competition was complete, many of the jockeys would go to a local night club to party to unwind then go home take some prescribed sleeping pills and then repeat the same pattern all over again the next day.

The jockey's world is closed to most people and you are only let in by invitation once you have earned their trust. It was an honor to have been allowed into their world and I spent two years working the Los Alamitos Racing Season. Being true to the jockey's code, I choose not to talk about the controversial practices that I observed while I was working there, but I can assure you that these individuals where admirable, dedicated and always trying to win.

By the third season I did not have the time to work at the track anymore. After all, my first son had just been born and I wanted to be home when I could, so I recommended one of my student trainers from Golden West, a man named Jack Steele for the race track job and he then took over.

Jack was an interesting character. He was a Juvenal Diabetic that totally abused his body. He loved to party, hangout with the ladies, and drink. The last vice, drinking, is defiantly not recommended for diabetics because it is a fast track to death for them. Over the years Jack began to change his lifestyle because he knew his body was starting to deteriorate. His life saving moment came when he met a wonderful woman named Carol who he would end up marrying and I was graciously blessed to be the best man in their wedding ceremony. Not too long after their nuptials Jack found out his kidneys were beginning to fail and the only way to preserve his life was going to be dialysis while the search went on for a transplant donor. Jack was adopted as a child, so finding a match was going to be like looking for the proverbial needle in a haystack. As Jack prepared for dialysis he told his wife that he thought they should move out of state to Arizona where the company she worked for was offering her a promotion if they moved there. The move was prompted by the fact that Jack and Carol had recently had a baby girl and he wanted security for them in case he didn't live. It was discussed at length by them and decided they would move there for her job security.

As the months went by and the futile search went on looking for a kidney donor, the most remarkable thing happened, the found a perfect match! For the first time in history it was discovered Jacks perfect donor was his own wife. Can you imagine that; it truly had to be a marriage that was arranged by God himself. A moment ago when I told you that when Jack met Carol it was a life saving moment, you just took me literally didn't you!

Soon after the donor match testing was complete, the surgery was performed and the transplant worked beautifully. To this day Jack, Carol and their daughter live in Kingman Arizona and Jack works for the county as a nutritionalist who informs people on proper dietary eating habits to prevent the onset of heart disease, strokes and of course to help minimize the effects of diabetes.

With the 1975 football season approaching, I was excited. We now had a full blown sports medicine staff in place, including great doctors, strong hospital alliances and a full staff of student assistants. All that was left to do was for me to take the wheel and direct the ship. For the next several years our reputation as a great sports medical team grew in Orange County CA. As our programs reputation grew, so did the demand for our time. Dr. Cassidy and I were always being asked to participate at sports medicine conferences, hospital workshops and even radio and television sports talk shows. It was flattering, but it only drove me to work harder to prove my worth as a professional and a Polio survivor.

During that time frame Dr. Cassidy and I treated a vast array of sports injuries. Often times while I was attending sporting events or practices I would have to respond to on the field emergencies when a player became injured. I would like to point out one thing to you, no matter what the extent of the injury would be, the scream for help was the same. It was only one word and I heard it hundreds of times; that word was, "***CHIP***". Some of the injuries were minor, but many were serious and some were life threatening, and no matter what, I had to be prepared to react to the unknown.

Of all the injuries I treated over the years, from compound fractures to ruptured spleens, one particular instance sticks out more than others in my mind. We were playing a local community college in their home stadium, and before the game started I noticed they bench areas had sideline tarps down on the ground to keep the area turf from getting torn up. These ground covers came out from the benches all the way to the sidelines, and they covered the entire area between the two 30 yard line markers. The tarps were held in place with long giant nails with heads on them about the size of a dime. Some of the nails adjacent to the sidelines were not flush with the ground; they were sticking up, resembling a large golf tee placed in the ground. Dr. Cassidy and I went to the officials and expressed our concern and the head referees response was "Play the game or forfeit". There wasn't much we could do but play. Throughout the evening the players, the coaches and my staff would step on the exposed nails pushing them back into the ground. During one of the plays in the third quarter, one of our receivers stretched out and dove to catch a football near our sidelines. Seconds after the play I hear "***Chip***" and I ran over to assist the player. When I got there he was lying on his back, his left leg was bent normally at the knee, but on the front of his calf, half way between his knee and ankle, was a large 5 or 6 inch gash laying wide open and exposing the underlying muscles. It was quit the sight to see his muscles move and function with no tissue over them. Immediately I cleaned the area with sterile water and put a dressing on it to keep it as clean as possible for the trip to the emergency room. A few weeks after the incident, that injured player, who returned to play for us within a month, filed a lawsuit. Named in the case was the host college, the game officials and Golden West College! Why us? Because we knew there was the potential for danger and we played the game anyway. I was an expert witness used during the trail that settled early on, but that legal case, forever changed the protocol used at all football games.

Now, Officials' must take the responsibility to protect athletes from any potential hazards brought to their attention.

As the 1970's started to blend into the 1980's two things were apparent; I was successful as a trainer, and I was beginning to feel stagnant. It was at that time a long time physical therapist friend of mine by the name of Bruce Heckman approached me with a fresh new idea. He wanted the two of us to start a program that allowed individuals that had suffered strokes, heart attacks, and other disease entities to come to my small athletic training facility and continue rehabilitation programs after their insurance coverage was exhausted. It was an interesting idea, after all the college athletes were generally in class in the morning and my work load was lite in the morning. With Bruce's therapy background and with my knowledge and the fact that I dealt with my own disability, it seemed like a great match and so we began. We called the plan the Rehabilitation Fitness Program, and we started with 7 senior citizens who were all motivated to improve their personal fitness and stamina. The cost of operation for the program was minimal because my salary was already being paid by the college and there was no cost for the facility. The only charge was $30.00 a month to make it worth Bruce's time and believe me that cost was nothing considering that the participants could come in between 8:00am and 11:00am Monday thru Friday. Bruce and I would tailor the workouts to the needs and desires of each participant and the regiment of exercises helped them make gains toward a set goal. It was amazing to see the smiles on their faces each time one of them would realize an improvement in their physical well being. Along with the health improvements of each individual, the participants turned to each other and before you know it, they became one large support group. They, as a group, would request to have potluck gatherings during the year to celebrate as a family. This group of survivors were brought together by our program and ended up bonding and believing in each other for a far greater cause, overcoming adversity.

For some reason I became the leader and voice of the group. When they wanted to have their opinions heard on campus or in the community they would come to me for guidance and leadership. It changed my outlook on my future dramatically; I was no longer a Polio survivor trying to prove myself, I was the driving force carrying the banner for the entire local disabled community. I was not going to let them down, so I had to learn how to blend the rehabilitation program and my athletic training assignment into a seamless match. This group of physically disabled individuals added a heartwarming aspect to my job, but I was about to get spread too thin, and something was going to have to give way. I didn't realize it at the time, but that something was going to be my personal relationships.

CHAPTER
12

All though I was expanding my responsibilities to include the rehabilitation program, I did not lose my passion for athletic training. In fact in 1984 I was going to add to my experiences once again. A good friend of mine named Jim Noud, who was a Licensed Physicians Assistant, came to me with a desire to work with the upcoming Los Angeles Summer Olympics. I really wasn't interested because my second son had just been born, but Jim pleaded with me to get involved because most of the positions for the events were taken, and he knew I had connections with the USA Olympics Committee Members that were choosing the medical staff. Reluctantly I made a call to one of the committee members to check out what athletic events still needed coverage. To my surprise, they offered me two spots working with whatever sport I wanted to volunteer for. I called my buddy Jim back and ask him which sport would he like to work with? His immediate response was "Boxing" and so it was, the summer of 84 was coming and I was heading to work the medical coverage at the Olympics, and although I wasn't planning on working the event, it ended up that I'm glad I did.

All of the individuals that participated in the Los Angeles venues were given wonderful memorabilia to mark being part of this remarkable worldwide event. The uniforms, proclamation and collectors' items

I was presented with, I wrapped up and stored away to give to my 3 sons later in their lives.

Working at the boxing training venue was where I spent most of my time during both weeks of the competition and it was the best place to be. All of the participating countries would bring their teams to the facility to train and prepare. It allowed us to sit and talk with the boxers when they weren't under pressure or stressed out like they would be just before competing at the Sports Arena. Over at the training center I had the opportunity to spend time talking with future boxing champions Pernell Whitaker, Mark Breland and Evander Holyfield. All three of these men were very friendly and genuine people who were interested in hearing about my past history.

At one point, star boxer Mark Breland, a member of the USA contingent stopped working out with the team and started working out with a private promoter. Our team coach Pat Nappi who had coached the USA team for years, was devastated by the situation. The disagreement between the two men was being esculated by the press coverage and especially by television sporting news celebrity Howard Cosell. One day, when my buddy Jim and I were the only ones working at the training site, a highly publicized conflict came to a head. Coach Nappi walked into our training room and collapsed. Immediately Jim and I were faced with the life threatening situation. We placed the coach on a treatment table began resuscitation and stabilized him as we waited for paramedics to respond. The coach was transported to the hospital for treatment where he recovered from diabetic complications. What was interesting was the follow up news reports, including the ABC report filed by Howard Cosell, did not resemble what really happened at the time. The truth is Jim and I did keep the coach from slipping into a diabetic coma and we protected him from dying.

As for Jim and I; before the adrenaline rush from the occurrence could subside, we were approached by athletes preparing for competition and in need of medical assistance. Oh well, back to work, after all it was just another day in the life of an athletic trainer.

Quickly my working life returned to my normal responsibilities after my Olympic experience. The growth of the Rehabilitation Program at the college was very apparent, because Bruce and I started with 7 people, but now the word was out and we had grown to 30 plus participants. We could no longer continue to operate out of the small facility, so it was time for me to promote the program to the college administration, the district trustee members and to our community leaders. Not only would I go throughout the community to promote the service we were offering, but now the hospitals, physicians and therapist were sending us patients and we weren't asking them to. Once people realized the importance and uniqueness of the program, the time was right to ask for a new facility.

I would have never been able to get a new building constructed to serve the sports programs, but the Rehab. Program was a different story. The need for that particular cliental pulled on people's heartstrings and the athletes were going to benefit. With renderings of a facility I had drawn in hand, I went to the college president and sat down to talk with him. In our discussion I said one thing, "If you want me to keep running the Rehabilitation Program we need a new building to properly serve the clients, and here is what I want", and I then handed him my rendering. Understand this, I had done my homework and I already had the backing of powerful people in the district who I had built relationships with over the years. Even though it appeared that I went in and brought up my request to the president cold turkey, the ball was in motion long before my meeting. During that visit and a few minutes after the president looked over my renderings he looked up at me and said "you've got it". As I walked out of his office, I knew that all the relationships I had built over the years within the district had paid off. For the first time in the college history, an individual was able to convince the administration to make a truly major commitment based on one persons conviction, and that person was little old me.

As the anticipation and excitement about getting a new facility started to grow inside me, we still needed to get through the early part of 1985 without it. The athletic training side of things was on autopilot because of my great support staff headed up by Kyle Kawabata. Kyle was an individual that thought a lot like I did, worked extremely hard and most important of all, he was dedicated to me. That made it easy because I could concentrate on issues concerning the Rehab. Program and the new building while Kyle over saw the daily operation of the sports medicine side of our program.

One day, while I was working with the rehabilitation patients, I noticed one of our stroke survivors trying to get onto a treadmill to walk. Now think of this; at that point in our society, most treadmills were designed to either be going at a selected speed, or not at all. An able body person could easily straddle the moving belt, time the pace of the movement and then step on. That was not so easy for a stroke patient with leg and arm movement restrictions. When these weary individuals would attempt to step on the rapidly moving belt, it was difficult at best and of course their big concerned was about falling down. Soon they would get frustrated and give up on the ordeal. It was at that point in time I decided to do research and see if there were machines available that would work for our participants needs. I discovered that there was a treadmill on the market that would work quit well for us, but it was expensive. This particular machine allowed our patients to stand right in the middle of the treadmill track, turn it on and the belt would start moving very slowly until it got up to whatever the chosen speed was. It was perfect! The only problem was how were we going to pay for it? It was at that time I had an idea, it was a thought that would rely on one of my old talents and once again I must get buy in by certain individuals on campus.

It is time to pause again and interject another thought that never crosses most people's minds. I can't tell you how many times I've had friends tell me that they just think of me as a normal guy. They'll say "I don't even notice your limp". To them, that is a great thought and a compliment, and I truly understand that. What I'm thinking when someone makes that comment is; thanks, but you don't know how hard it is to make it look like this.

Let me try and explain it this way. Years ago Dr. Cassidy wanted me to go and see a famous orthotic brace maker and have him design and fit me with a custom knee brace with the hope that it would improve my walking. In my particular case, when walking, I use my right hand and press lightly on the front of my upper right thigh, there by stabilizing my leg to support my body weight.

The day I went to the orthotic's office; they took me into a large examination room and asked me to strip down to the shorts I was wearing. The specialist came in and asks me to walk across the room and then walk back, and so I did. He carefully studied how I moved and when I walked back up to him he said "I can't mess with perfection". He went on to say that I have perfected where to push with my hand to stabilize my hip, lockout my knee, and place my foot in the right position. All of that thought process and mechanical movement taking place in a millisecond.

Another example of adapting is when I sit down and I go to cross my right leg over my left one, the motion looks normal to most people, but in actuality I am using my hand to bump my leg up and over with a quick timed push.

I cannot speak on the specifics that other disabled individuals use to adapt to participate in mainstream society, but I can say this; People will study a video of a professional golfers swing to try improve their own motion. They then will practice and practice to try and get it right. Most of the time, these individuals may come close to achieving what they want, as they try and achieve ultimate perfection. When someone puts in all those hours to learn and perfect their swing, often times the effort is recognized by their friends and colleagues. The individual that has made the golf swing improvement thinks, you don't know how hard it was to get to this point, and that is how a disabled person thinks too. Many hours are invested by disabled people perfecting their ability to walk, get in out of the car, or write with a pen. To me, the most important thing to remember is to appreciate the extraordinary skill developed by an individual that has adapted to their disability.

Hey, it's not easy making things look as normal as possible.

Once again let's return to my story.

The idea I had for raising money for the rehabilitation program was simple. Put on a variety show in the college theater, sell tickets and use the proceeds to purchase the treadmill. There was a problem, you can't just use the theater on campus, I would need an accomplished director and I would need a number of individuals with theater technical skills to volunteer to work the event.

The first step was getting a polished performance director with the skills, knowledge and patience to teach me how to put on a show.

That task was fairly easy. Stu Rodgers was the department chair of our theater department and guess what; he loved to workout in our weight room.

From time to time Stu would suffer a minor injury and he would come in to see me about rehabilitating his damaged body part. I knew if I got his buy in, the rest could happen. I went over to his office and explained what my plan was and with no hesitation, he bought in.

The next thing I knew we were in production meetings with all the theater specialists we needed and all of them willing to volunteer. We came up with a name for the show "Let Us Entertain You" and we started looking for acts. We ended up with a mix of employees, students and as I recall a clown that made balloon animals. Oh yeah, there was also me. I was going to play my guitar, sing and be the co-master of ceremonies with Stu. Let me tell you, wonderful experience it turned out to be. It raised enough money to purchase the new treadmill and it brought much needed notoriety to the program.

For the next few years we put on the show raising money to buy new and better equipment for the Rehabilitation Program and throughout the experience, I was learning the art of stage production from Stu.

I did not know at the time, but because of those acquired producing/directing skills I now possessed, a few years later I would be asked to put on a whole new series of shows renamed "Over the Rainbow" and those shows would benefit a whole new set of causes.

While we began to move into our new facility in 1986, I found out that I was selected by the National Athletic Trainers Association to be recognized as the top Community College Trainer in the United States. It was a huge honor and I did not take it lightly. My then wife and I were flown back to the East Coast for 3 days where I received the award. It was a wonderful experience, complete with all the pomp and circumstance that accompanies such an honor.

Upon returning home, I received a very interesting phone call a few days later. The call was from a man that said he read in the paper about me receiving the award. He went on to say how proud he was of my accomplishments and he wondered if I would help him rehabilitate his surgically repaired knee. I thanked him for the compliment and told him we could help him rehab his knee through the Rehabilitation Fitness Program. As we chatted, it became more apparent that the man on the phone knew about my past and after a short while he said, "I bet you wonder who this is, I'm Bailey Duarte". At that point my jaw dropped and my heart swelled. If you take the time to look back in the book, you will find that Bailey Duarte was the high school basketball coach that over 20 years earlier took me out of the adaptive physical education class and introduced me to athletic training. Imagine, I owed that man the world and all he was asking for was a little assistance.

Once he had successfully completed his rehabilitation regiment working out with me, it was time for him to leave us. That day he walked over to me and said "Chip thank you for taking the time to help me". I looked at him and said "No coach, thank you for believing in me so many years ago. It was your belief and you taking the time to care, that put me on the road to potential success".

At that moment we shook hands and he turned to walk out the door, still not realizing the importance and impact he had made on my life.

Thanks Coach!

During the next few years life in the new facility was very challenging. We were attracting many new participants for the Rehabilitation Program, the sports medicine side of my responsibilities continued to be demanding and it seemed there wasn't enough of me to go around. Not only was I working with the athletes and rehabilitation students, I was constantly looking for ways to purchase more equipment to better serve all of them. I was going into the community to promote the program and of course I was continuing the variety show. There was one big difference for the upcoming 5th show, my friend and mentor, Stu Rodgers, had retired and I was left to gather the talent, produce, direct, perform, and be master of ceremonies. Thank heaven Stu had taught me the skills required to put a show together and for the new show I asked our college president Judith Valles to be my co-master of ceremony and she graciously accepted. Not to sound conceded, but the next two years, with her working with me on stage, the shows continued to be tremendous successes.

Mean time, while we generated money to buy equipment to better serve our students, I had my eye on a rehabilitation device that my variety show couldn't generate enough funds for. The machine could perform finite measurements in muscle strength and weaknesses and would assist patients perform their exercises. The problem was it cost $50,000 and I needed big time help for that one. I went to our college foundation office and presented my case. Before you know it I had outside donors coming into the rehabilitation center to observe our operations and ask questions. Within a few weeks I got a call from the head of the foundation telling me that a wealthy donor was moved by the rehabilitation student's determination to overcome their disabilities and that benefactor would pay the entire cost for the machine. I had to pinch myself. We were going to have a machine that most medical clinics couldn't afford to buy and we were just a small college program with a lot of determination.

Yes, our program was firing on all cylinders, but things were about to take a dramatic change that would end one program, change the face of the other one and there was nothing I could do to prevent it!

CHAPTER
13

The 1994 school year started off the same as any other year. My mornings were busy with rehabilitation students and in the afternoons I was inundated with injured athletes.

As we progressed through the football season it was late in the second half of the game against Cerritos College and I was standing up close to the sidelines. During a play, in which our star running back was carrying the football, he suddenly turned and started running in my direction. When I realized what was happening I tried to move to my left and right but both those routes were blocked off by some of our players standing on either side of me. As I went to step back, one of my assistants thought I was falling backwards so they pushed me forward, and at the same moment the Golden West Player was pushed from behind forcing him out of bounds.

The next thing I remember was flying through the air with the player grabbing me around the waist and concurrently I was trying to turn my upper body to catch myself with my arms and cushion the fall. It seemed like everything was happening in slow motion as we flew about 20 feet before hitting the ground. As I put my hands out to prepare for the landing and with all the twisting of my body I felt and heard a loud "POP" in my lower back. That was it, in a split second my training career was over. Even though I didn't realize it at the moment, within a few days the doctors would determine that I would no longer have the ability to carry out the daily requirements necessary for a trainer. I couldn't believe it, after years of education and experience it was over. At that point and with very little ceremony I was relieved of my responsibilities as the colleges' athletic trainer.

As I was recovering from lower back surgery, the college and district administrators were contemplating with to do with me when I returned. To my disbelief, the decision that the district leadership came to was not only unique, but for that time, it was unheard of.

When I returned to work at the college a month or so later, I was called into the vice president's office to discuss my working future. At that time the vice president was Dr. Fred Owens, the same man that originally hired me as the trainer 20 years earlier. He told me that the decision was made to have me train and become the athletic academic advisor. At the same time the district was willing to send me back to school to earn my Masters Degree in Educational Counseling if I wanted to go. Of course I was willing to take advantage of the offer. So for the next 2 ½ years I would work with the athletes helping build their class schedules, keep them on track to graduate and oh yes, I would go to school at night and on weekends to earn my masters degree. It was a busy time.

During that time period I helped many athletes achieve academic success, but one particular individual sticks out way above the rest.

Van Tuinei was a local high school football player who was big, strong, and fast. The only problem was he was the leader of a major local gang. The first time I ever met him was when he enrolled in a sports medicine class I was teaching before I was hurt. He was still in high school at the time but wanted to see what college was like. When he would show up to class, he was always wearing a heavy coat, a stocking cap pulled down over his ears and he always set in the back corner facing the door.

One evening, after class, I started talking with him about his persistence about wearing that heavy coat. He said to me "you don't want to know what I'm carrying under it". As we continued our conversation Van expounded on his gang involvement and I came to find out he wasn't in a gang, he ran it! Before the end of that spring semester, Van disappeared and didn't return to class.

A few years later in 1995, I was sitting in my office, settling into my new advisors position and in walks Van. He came up to me and asked if he could sit down. Of course I said yes and at that time we began to talk. The first question out of my mouth was, where have you been? He looked me in the eyes and shared the following story.

As the end of that spring semester, when he was attending my class, the gang pressure on him ratcheted up and his girlfriend gave birth to a son belonging to Van. Wanting to do the right thing for his new family he knew he would have to distance himself from the gang and police. With that in mind he took his girlfriend and their new son to Seattle to restart their lives. Van got a job at the airport as a luggage handler and they settled in. Soon gang members were getting in touch with him asking that he consider selling drugs up in that northern region. As Van contemplated the idea for making that easy money, his girlfriend gave birth to their second child, a little girl. That's all it took, once Van saw her he wanted nothing to do with any illegal activities, and he took a second job in a major hotel setting up and tearing down tables, chairs and other equipment required for banquets and other events. He was happy with his new life.

One day when Van was at work, he got a call from the local hospital telling him to come over right away. Upon arrival at the hospital he found his little girl had died of SIDS (Sudden Infant Death Syndrome). As the reality sunk in, no longer did Van want anything to do with his jobs or Seattle, so he packed up his family and once more moved back home to Westminster CA.

Once he was back he was torn between his gang affiliations and his desire to do the right thing. Van was so stressed out that he knew he needed to relieve his frustration, but how was he going to do that. His way of reducing stress was by lifting weights, and the only place he knew that he could go to work out in a weight room was Golden West College, a place he was familiar with. That's when he came and saw me.

As we sat there and continued our conversation I asked him had he thought about still playing football. After all he still was eligible to play, so why not. He laughed, rolled his eyes and got up to leave. I asked him to really think about it as he walked out the door. A few days later he returned and said he had talked it over with his family and he was going to try and play. I told him that I would help him build his class schedule around practice and a part time job, and if he was willing to listen to my suggestions, when the time came for him to go on and play football at the university level he would be ready.

Two years quickly passed, I was finishing my master's degree and Van was finishing his football career at Golden West. We both had done what we needed to do in the classroom, so it was time to see what the results were going to be from all our work. Well, because of Van's skills on the field and his diligence in the classroom he was offered a full scholarship to the University of Arizona. I was so proud of him I put him up for an award offered to athletes that have overcome adversity to succeed. Van won in a landslide and I remember as the two of us set at the awards ceremony Van leaned over to me and whispered, "I've never sat at a banquet table before, I've set plenty of them up, but I've never actually sat at one". I smiled and whispered back "you deserve it my friend".

Just so you know, Van went on to play for the University of Arizona, followed by the San Diego Chargers, Indianapolis Colts and Chicago Bears. He has now settled with his family in Indianapolis. One last note a year ago, in 2008, Van called me and said he was going to send his son to come and play at Golden West and he ask me to counsel and watch over his son while he was here and so I did. His son played for us for one year. He took care of business on the field and in the classroom and after that first year, he left on an athletic scholarship to the University of Oregon.

It was during that year in 1995, while I was working with Van, I learn how wonderful the feeling was to help direct someone towards future success. At that time, as I was preparing to graduate with my Masters Degree in Educational Counseling, I had no idea of the positive impact I was going to be making on the lives of hundreds of future students.

CHAPTER
14

In the month of January1997 I was about to make a dramatic change in my working carrier. For the first time in my adult life I was going to have a job outside of an athletic department. The chancellor of our district approached me and offered me a fulltime faculty position as a counselor in the EOPS/CARE Department. The last thing he said to me at the time was "Make me proud of this decision". Now just like most of you reading this, I'm thinking what the heck is EOPS?

EOPS (Extended Opportunity Programs and Services) is a program that is offered by all the California Community Colleges and fund by the state. The program offers an array of specialized services to students that are educationally and financially challenged when they enter community college. With the additional services that are offered, the EOPS programs throughout the State of California consistently prove to have higher student success rates then the general student population. The CARE Program (Cooperative Agencies Resources for Education) is an offshoot of EOPS and is aimed at serving single parents with young children and they are on public financial assistance. I came into the department as a counselor but it wasn't long before I was elected as the director in charge of running the program. When I started in EOPS, we had 750 students annually. I'm proud to say since I took over running the program it has grown to 1,300 participants. I have to say my leadership skills have had a lot to do with the dramatic increase.

At first it seemed like a pretty tame job, but then I started to learn the stories of the students; tails of spousal abuse, abandonment, and broken families. Many of the stories are heart wrenching, but two specific students stories that I was involved with, especially come to my mind.

One day while I was sitting my offices on of the EOPS Counselors came into my office, set down by my desk and said to me that she had a student in her office that just made an unusual request and didn't know how to handle it. The counselor went on to say that the 31 year old female student had just stated that she is a single Vietnamese Mom, she has no relatives in the United States, she was just diagnosed with terminal cancer and she wanted what was going to happen to her 8 year old daughter. The student was terrified that her young daughter would be lost in the foster youth system. I looked over at the counselor and said, "I'll start making some phone calls". As I started querying people three things kept coming up; talk with the local press, talk with the local churches and talk with the local politician's. I immediately jumped in my van drove over to the state assemblyman's office to have a chat. During my visit the assemblyman and his staff seemed most interested in helping and before you knew it radio shows, local television news shows and the local press were putting out the word. The response was overwhelming and it wasn't long before a family match was found to adopt the child. As sad as the final outcome was for the mother, she found some peace before she died in knowing her daughter was going to be taken care.

Another example concerns one of our EOPS/CARE students. Our CARE Counselor walked into my office and said the one of her students, a single mom and her child who were on public assistance, had become homeless and they were living in a storage unit. The manager of the facility had caught them sneaking in one night and was going to turn the mother over to Child Protection Services. The mother was in a panic and had the weekend to straighten things out. The counselor and I loaded the mother and child into my van and started going to the local churches. It's funny because this happened on a Friday and every church we went to did not work with homeless issues on Fridays. How crazy is that! Sorry, don't become homeless on the weekend, we can't help you. As we continued to drive around we stopped and got something to eat and the counselors' phone rang. When she answered the individual said that our student could stay with her through the weekend and went on to say the other CARE Students had pooled some of their very limited monetary resources and paid the first month's rent on a place for the mom and daughter to live.

Those are examples of the kind of student population I know work with. The thing is, those two stories can be multiplied by the hundreds over the past 12 years. I truly was placed in a position where I made a much bigger impact on society than I ever had in the past. Before I made a difference in individual's lives, now I help made a difference in society.

As I was learning, enjoying and expanding my new assignment at the college, one more time I was going to presented with a new hurdle, and it was going to be the shock of my life.

It was the fall of 2005 and I was getting a routine physical at the office of our team physician. As he was reviewing my blood test results he mentioned that my PSA was elevated and he wanted me to make an appointment with a urologist for a follow up study. I said I would and I left. A couple of weeks later I made the appointment and went in. The urologist was a little concerned about the blood work and ordered a prostate biopsy. The test was done and within a few days I received a call to come to the office and bring my sons with me. When we got to the office, the secretary escorted us back into a very posh office. I knew what I was going to hear wasn't going to be good news; I just was unclear on what the outcome was going to be. When the doctor walked in and set down as his desk, he told me and the boys it was not good. I had a very aggressive cancer and if I didn't do something very soon the cancer would start to spread throughout my body quickly. He went on to talk about the treatment options, but in my case he recommended open surgery so he could make sure it had not spread. I was disappointed, but my boys took it very hard, they didn't want to lose their dad. The next thing I know I'm in the hospital recovering from the tricky surgery. The nurses said I set a record for getting out of the hospital following that type of surgery; I went home in 2 days.

Over the years, while I was recovering from all the corrective surgeries I went through, I learned two things; I wanted out of the hospital fast and the only way to do it was to mask the pain and tell the nurses it didn't hurt, so that's what I have always done. For me the trick to help with pain manage is this, I concentrate on the pain and in my mind I make it hurt as much as possible, then when I stop thinking about it, it doesn't hurt as bad. It's that simple but for me very effective. At any rate, on that second day following surgery I was leaving the hospital and heading home.

After a few weeks of recovery I was back at work helping students, but the problem with that in retrospect was, no one was helping me. I didn't need help with the physical recovery, but the psychological recovery was and is a different story. Not being married, I had no one of the opposite sex to help me rebuild my feelings of self worth as a viable partner and it is an issue that I deal with to this day. I often think if I had it to do over again, I wouldn't have the surgery, sure it saved my life, but at what cost; I don't feel complete as a man and oh how important that is to me. At any rate my life was saved and I am a successful cancer survivor, whoopee, big deal.

One of the saddest situations I ever encountered in my adult life happen at Golden West to one of our long time college football coaches. His name was Dennis Dixon and he often would come in to visit with me. One day he came in my office and showed me the palm of his right hand and you could see where the muscles were starting to deteriorate. I immediately referred him to one of our team doctors for evaluation. A few weeks later the word came to me that he was suffering with Amyotrophic Lateral Sclerosis (ALS) and it was terminal. For the next few months he and I talked often; I think it was because I was disabled and he now felt I could relate to his problems. As his condition worsened he had to retire and soon after that he was hospitalized. Within a few months, we were attending his funeral and I had the honor to help eulogize him. In my comments I told the overflow congregation about the respect he had developed for the disabled community when he became part of it. He wanted me to implore people not to over look the worth of the disabled and to recognize their value individually, not to judge them as a whole segment of society.

When the service was over, Dennis's family thanked me and a reporter from the Los Angeles Times came over and asked me if he could quote me in the paper. I told them "use the words but attribute the quote to the rightful owner, Dennis Dixon".

As time passed by, I always wanted to do something to honor Dennis, and I finally got my chance. There was going to be a local 5K Walk to benefit the ALS Association. Now, at this point of my life, my physical health has began to deteriorate and I don't walk very well anymore, but I was determined to be part of the event. So, I gathered a few friends and family members, collected over a $1,000 in donations and headed to the walk.

When we got there a large group had already gathered at the starting line as I passed by to turn in the money. Soon the gun went off and the walk began and the crowd began to spread out as they crossed over the starting line. Later that morning the walkers began to return from the course and naturally the group had thinned as they journeyed the route, but there in the back, far from the lead was me, on my crutches. As I crossed the finish line, I remember looking up to the sky and saying out loud "rest in peace my friend".

Even though I myself was left with a major physical affliction, you should recognize by now I have been dedicated to helping individuals overcome the personal adversities they face. I've worked with those struggling to adjust to physical barriers presented to them because of a disease or misfortune, and I've worked with groups that face hardship because of social and financial barriers while pursuing an education. All of these individuals are deserving of such support.

Recently, I've become involved with a cause that I see as greater than the rest, "Emancipated Foster Youth". It 's ironic that turning 18 years old in the USA means you're emancipated, because all it does is release you from being the responsibility of the foster care system. At 18 years old, you no longer have guaranteed housing, transportation, food or health service support. Over 25% of these young people end up homeless, more than 20% end up in prison and less than 1% can afford to attend and graduate from a college, university or trade school.

Here at Golden West College I have brought together a group of individuals that are dedicated to making a difference for this under represented part of our society. Together we are addressing the needs of Southern California Foster Youth who are pursuing their higher education goals. Our expert volunteers hear the tragic stories of abuse and neglect that our students have faced. We look into their eyes when they tell us about their homelessness, transportation issues or the fact that they haven't eaten for days. Yet they still come to our college possessing nothing more than hope. They want to overcome the barriers and they fight to succeed. Unfortunately, for many of them the obstacles are overwhelming and they are forced to give up.

This is by far the biggest challenge I've ever faced. To build trust with a group of individuals that have been brought up not trusting anyone and to instill in them the motivation to overcome. Although their challenges may seem insurmountable, as you know by now I'm not one that gives up easily. I will fight whole heartedly for their cause, so let the battle begin. We involved at Golden West will make a difference, I promise you.

In closing this part of my book I would like to say, I know that my professional life will soon be coming to an end; so I would like to propose a toast! Not to the accomplishments I have realized in my life, but to all the individuals that helped me achieve them. I only hope that their memories of the important part they have played in my life are half as strong as the gratitude I have for all of them for being part of it.

Cheers!

CHAPTER
15

This section of my book will revolve around three major obstacles I wanted to conquer, water skiing, riding a motorcycle, and snow skiing.

Water Skiing

When I was young the Wilson family and my family would go to Lake Havasu every summer. At that time the lake was little known and no developments like today. Everyone in our group would try and ski, but the few times I tried I would lose control of my weak leg and I was unsuccessful. After not succeeding for a couple of years, I decided to stop trying because I was wasting their time and the time that other people could ski. I told myself, my day will come.

1970 was a new time in my river life. My parents had bought a large mobile home at a marina in Arizona at a place called Temple Bar. A new day was coming, because at that same time I bought my first boat. It was a 14ft piece of junk that seated three people and was not fast. The only thing that mattered is that it was mine and I had control over it. Every summer I would take multiple trips with large groups of friends and multiple boats out there. One day I asked two of my closest friends to pull me behind the boat while I attempted to get up on one ski. I knew I could never control two skis, so I was going to have to adapt dragging my weak right leg around like an anchor while I tried to get up. It was truly trial, error and perseverance. With the patience of my two friends, finally two hours later I got up out of the water and then fell. Not a great accomplishment to most people, but to my two friends and I it proved I would be able to do it.

Over the next few years as my boat and equipment changed I became accomplished as a water skier developing some skills others skiers couldn't imagine were possible. There was one thing I couldn't do that my close friends could however and that was shore starting. Shore starting is when you stand on one foot in ankle deep water, lift the ski up with the other foot and when the boat takes off, it pulls you into a skiing position without getting wet. I really wanted to try it, but how was I going to support my body weight on my weak leg while I held the ski up? I came up with an answer, a bar stool start.

By our next trip, I had a bar stool. When the time was right, I took it out into the water about two feet deep, set on it with my ski pointing in the right direction, and yelled "hit it" and bam face first into the mud of the shallow water. After repositioning the stool and attempting many more times on multiple trips, I gave up on it. Although I never got that one to work, it did go down in the archives' with my friends as one of the craziest things I ever tried but more shocking to them was I didn't get it to work.

A few years later, I invited an amputee snow skiing group out to the lake that I met at a function I put on at the college. I was going to teach them all how to water ski. To my surprise 7 of them, a mix of men and women, showed up eager to learn. 6 of them were missing legs and one was missing an arm. By that time I was an accomplished skier and instructor. I'll never forget the first day when I took them out on the water and I glanced to the back of my boat and I saw 6 prosthetic legs standing there. It warmed my heart that they trusted me enough to come out and try to learn to ski.

As the day progressed, my friend Leonard Schulz and I worked with each of them individually, all of them succeeded, except one, the one armed individual. It was a lady who had her arm ripped off as a young child inside an old style washing machine. From the beginning we decided to put her on two skis because it would be better for her balance and less drag trying to get up. After a couple of attempts she said it was impossible and she wanted to quit. I quickly asked her, if I get in and get up on one foot with one arm will you keep trying? She reluctantly said yes. So I got in the water put on my ski, grabbed the rope with one hand, yelled "hit it" and away I went. When I returned to the beach, she once again gave it a couple tries but did not succeed.

That evening as we set around, I played my guitar and everyone was bragging about their success. The one armed lady seemed somewhat depressed. I said to her, you played the game that's all that counts. She said what do you mean? I then told the group I had written a song about being disabled and I sang it for them. They loved it, because it's all about getting involved.

Now that group of individuals was a very accomplished snow skiing group that competed internationally. After I sang the song, they ask me to please come to the National Amputee Ski Championships in Aspen in the fall and perform it at the banquet. Like an idiot, I declined because I was dedicated to my training job during that time of year.

I'm going to take a moment here. This may not be the right place, and it won't be the same without the music, but I guess this is as good as place as any to share the words to that song.

We may be walking in a funny way
We may be talkin in a funny way
But no matter what you think of me, I'm going to make you see
That as a person I am free
I like to wander and to move around
There's only one thing that can hold me down

*My inabilities to open up my mind
And leave inhibitions behind
So come and walk with me as I move along
I think that you may find your thoughts are wrong
Although I'm different, really no one is the same
It's all in how you play the game.*

Guess what; to this day I still boat at Temple Bar.

When I was sixteen years old I wanted to try and ride a motorcycle. I learned to ride a bicycle so how much harder could it be. The problem was no one was going to let me try and learn on their bikes, so I had to talk my parents in to buying me one. I'm not sure how I convinced them, but my father researched the subject and found a motorcycle that he thought would work for me. It was a Honda 55 that had an automatic transmission and a rear brake pedal on the left side (the side of my strong leg).

Soon I was trying my luck riding down the street in front of my house on my Honda 55. It wasn't as hard as I thought it would be. I just had to learn to always keep my weight on my left leg when I stopped at a light or for any other reason. If for any reason I misplaced my balance on the motorcycle and ended up tipping to the right I could not catch myself and falling all the way to the street was the outcome. During all of my days of riding bikes falling like that would happen from time to time but it was more embarrassing than painful.

During that time in the 60's a state law was passed requiring a driver's license for riding motorcycles. I was going to have to take a test at the DMV to validate my skills. The day came for me to go and take the test and I was confident, after all I had been riding a while and had mastered the old 55. I took the written test which was a breeze and went out to take the riding test. As I walked outside, I noticed the DMV Evaluator looking at me funny. When it was my turn to ride, he said to me," what are you doing here? You shouldn't be riding a motorcycle with a handicap. Riding is way too dangerous for you". I explained to him I was confident in my riding and with a doubtful eye he let me begin. Now imagine having to impress a DMV employee that doubts your abilities before you even start, I was nervous. I got on my bike rode between the cones, stopped where and when I was suppose to and finished next to him. He looked at me and said, "I was sure you couldn't do it, here is your certificate". He then smiled and walked away. I guess I was making believer's one person at a time.

Over the years I graduated to bigger and bigger motorcycles. Some of them didn't have automatic starters, so if they died for whatever reason I had a problem. The kick starter was on the right side so I couldn't use my leg to start it, so I would reach down with my right arm and thrust as hard as I could on the kick starter. I was always able to get it to restart, although sometimes it didn't work the first time and at that point I would hear about it from the traffic backing up behind me.

I must admit that it was difficult and dangerous learning to ride and compensate to more powerful bikes, but determination helped to do it. Although I never did become an "Easy Rider", I did become competent and made many trips from Whittier to places like Palm Springs, Big Bear and multiple beach towns.

Snow Skiing,

I've attempted and accomplished some pretty difficult things in my life, but none were more difficult than snow skiing.

In 1968 snow skiing was getting popular with my crowd in East Whittier and I didn't want to be left out. I talked with my father and like he always did he researched the subject of disabled skiers. It is very impressive how he did that because there was no internet or home computers then. Anyway he discovered that in Europe there were amputee skiers that would use one ski and have runners on their poles. Somehow my father, who was an artist and designer, got some old ski poles and some old foot long ski tips and attached them together so all that was left to get was a ski a boot and a binding. I visited the local sporting goods store and I asked the salesman if they had any single skis where the second one may have been damaged in shipping. He went into the back storage room and came back out with a single wood ski old gold in color and ironically enough with big bold letters on it spelling "Unicorn". It definitely wasn't a popular brand, but it was made in Austria so I decided it must be good. I also bought some old lace up boots and bear trap bindings to complete my needs. After assembling everything, I knew I was ready to "hit the slopes". A couple of weeks later, as you should realize by now, my long time friend Leonard and I went up to Big Bear Mountain for our first skiing adventure.

My most vivid memory from that trip was standing in the snow lacing up my boots, walking up the slope about 100 feet, putting my ski on and balancing with those damn poles. About 150 downhill feet later I ended up with a broken leg when unable to stop, I crashed into a shed.

The next season I once again took to the mountain trying my luck on two skis, my Unicorn and a borrowed one. I also decided to use two regular poles because I felt they would aid me much better in stopping than a wall, tree, or those confounded outrunner poles.

This new idea was a disaster as well. As I started down the hill, the tip of the ski on my weak leg caught in some crusty powder and lacking the strength to pull it out of the snow, my legs went in opposite directions. This caused me to fall to my butt without bending my knees and dislocating my hip. Fortunately as I rolled over, in much discomfort, my hip popped back into the joint. As I laid there, no one was coming to my aid so I had to get up and slowly slide sideways back down the mountain.

Following that very short second season, the third season of snowfall was coming, and during the long layoff, I had developed a new strategy. I would use a regular ski on my good leg and short 30 inch ski on my weak one. The idea behind the short ski was I could allow it to ride on the snow, but it would be light enough for me to pull out of the powder.

In the beginning, my progress was poor. I need to stop here and explain something. In those days when you went to ski, you had three choices for ascending a slope, chairlifts, rope tows, or t-bars. Now for me rope tows and t-bars were not going to work. There are two uniform tracks in the snow where people placed their skis while going up the hill. Where was I to put my one ski that I was supporting my weight? Those two choices weren't going to work for me so that left one choice, the chair lift. If you didn't know back then, in California, the bunny slopes were always rope toe and t bars only, the chair lift was reserved for the BIG hills.

With limited confidence and lack of experience boarding a chair lift, I slowly made my way through the line to get on. When it was my turn, while I was attempting to sit down, I crossed my skis and while trying to uncross them, the tip of my short ski got caught in the snow. This caused a whipping effect throwing me face first into the snow and wedging, the back of the ski between the slats of the seat, much like wedging a toothpick vertically in your mouth. The other skiers waiting in line were very unhappy when they stopped the lift to dig me out. When I finally climbed back on the chair and got to the off ramp, I fell and slid down the ramp incline on my butt. When I stood up I felt relief, I had made it to where I needed to be, the top of a run!

As I stood there looking down the hill and all the trees, I pondered how I was going to make a right hand turn, avoiding the trees and a visit with the squirrels. I took a fearful breath, leaned forward, started to go, and to my surprise I was actually skiing. Now stopping was a different story. Unable to execute a proper turn, I purposely fell down to my right which faced me in the correct direction to continue. That first run was a long one, two and one half hours. It consisted of a trip here and a fall there and generally was an unpleasant experience. It was however an excellent run for learning to balance with the two skis and how to fall without getting hurt.

Once I got to the bottom of the hill I decided to call it a day. I was tired, sore and besides it was only the first day of a planned one week trip. After removing my skis and putting them in the rack, I headed for the lodge. My limp, an after effect from polio, was spotted by a woman member of the ski patrol. She ran over and said " have you been to the first aid station?" I puzzlingly said "why". She replied "because with a limp like that your leg has to be broken". It took a while but I finally convinced her I was alright, at which point she walked away looking disappointed that I wasn't maimed and in need of emergency care. I then knocked the snow off my boots, unzipped my jacket and went into the lodge to have a couple drinks to further numb my body.

As the day moved bye, the skiers began to come into the lodge, including my friends who had brought me on the trip and abandoned me on my first fall. They were all talking about their great runs, and of course I too made it sound like I had one great run after another. I guess I just didn't want them to know of my humiliation. At least that evening, as we set around a fondue relaxing my guitar playing and singing didn't embarrass me.

The next day as I reached the top of the lift, and after falling down the ramp once again, I spent a long time trying to evaluate how to make that first right hand turn. I cleared my mind, concentrated on the task at hand, and I took off sliding my Unicorns ski tail around. This caused me to make a c shaped right hand turn into a snow bank. This accomplishment was successful because by shifting my leg weight to my heel it brought the ski around allowing me to complete my first controlled turn, and I felt great!

Soon I was swishing (for lack of a better term) down the hills with my friends. I would head straight down the hill and when I couldn't go any farther, I would turn to my right to slow down and then purposely fall on my butt. Good old Leonard gave me the nickname of "Buns eye" Not because my runs were straight and fast, but because when I ran out of room I'd fall on my buns. Most people on the slopes would know where I was as they would here Leonard yelling "buns eye" as I barreled down a hill.

Then it happened, as I slid down a run in my typical style, I hit a mogul and my Unicorn was through. A complete break about one third of the way down from the tip. I hustled down to the ski shop and was able to purchase a single rental ski for $20.00. While examining the top surface of the ski and running my fingers over the cuts and gashes, I knew what must of happened to the skis mate. After a quick binding transplant, I was back on the slopes.

I became, by the loss of my Unicorn, much wiser. I knew that if I didn't learn to stop, the rental shop would run out of skis quickly. So, I took to the back hills and became a hermit. I was going to learn to stop on my ski bottoms, not mine. During my first attempts at developing a method of stopping, I would get up some speed, force the tip of my around to the right and then I would lean into the hill causing me to slide like a baseball player into second base. After a few attempts I discovered if I didn't force my ski around so violently, I could control the edges and stop maintaining my balance. After practicing a dozen or so times, I felt I should try some stops to my left, just in case at some future date a right hand turn is ruled out by a cliff, another skier, or too much wine from my bota bag.

The idea of stopping to the left was an interesting dilemma. The difficulty was I maintained almost all my weight on my left leg, and now how was I going to get a weighted ski to turn? On my first attempt I caught the inside edge of my ski and I took a fall. On my next try I dug in my outside edge of my ski, dragged my left pole in the snow and it worked, I stopped. Soon I was going down the mountain, turning left and right and stopping gracefully.

I suffered only one minor setback after that, I didn't know of the trap set by that the manufacturer of my poles. The latest ski pole baskets were multi-pointed, star shaped and made out of white plastic. The scheme was the manufacturer cleverly left off the lock washer that held the baskets on. So once as I dragged my left pole to stop, the basket came off. Try and find a white piece of plastic in a pure white snow bank. The rest of that run was lousy, planting a four foot spear into a ten foot snow base.

As soon as I got to the bottom of the hill I went to the ski shop, the Niemen/Marcus of the slopes, and purchase some bright blue baskets that could be seen if one cart wheeled off a pole. Along with the baskets I was given free two lock washers.

Once again I reemerged at the top of the run. I felt accomplished as I got off the chair without falling, and for the first time I felt like a real skier.

Over the years I went on to ski all over California and Colorado. Many times people would ask me about the short ski and depending on my mood I would tell them the truth or tell them it was a new kind of "trick ski". One time when I was up on a hill in Aspen a middle aged guy skied up to me, stopped and asked me about the skis. I was resting at the time so I told him the truth. He looked into my eyes and said, "How can you live? How can you drive a car? How can you do anything?" I thought about it for a second and then just skied off. Sometimes actions are better than words.

CHAPTER
16

Final Thoughts

Falling Down

Over the years I fell down a lot, and many times it was in public. Although many of my falls were upsetting, four come to mind as downright embarrassing.

When I was dating the lady that would become my first wife, we went to Disneyland for an outing. As we entered the park we moved through the crowd and made it to the main square. I was wearing blue jeans and had my hands in my pockets to conceal the fact that I was using my right hand to provide support for my walking. As I stepped off a curb, I lost my balance, fell to the street and in front of hundreds of people I rolled around trying to remove my hands from my pockets so I could get back up, not an easy task when you're wearing blue jeans. As a crowd gathered I heard someone yell "He's having a seizure". After what seems like an eternity, I finally got my hands out of my pockets and got back on my feet. Undaunted by the ordeal my date remained calm and was not upset by my incident.

When I got married for the first time, it was a beautiful backyard wedding. Between the rows of chairs was an attractively decorated carpeted aisle for the bride and groom to enter on. When it was my turn to pass down the aisle, as I got about halfway down, I stepped on a concealed sprinkler head and down I went, quickly I got back up.To this day I can still remember the gasps from the crowd as I tumbled to the ground.

The most embarrassing fall was when I was the best man in a friend of mines wedding. As I was sitting with him in church office before the ceremony, I told him that another guy and I had to light some candles prior to the groom coming down to the pulpit. I had never used one of those extended gold in color piece of ornate candle lighters that has a wick at the top to light the candles. I told him I was going to take a book of matches and put it in my vest just in case the flame went out. He laughed and said, "That never happens". Don't ever say never, because as I began raising the candle lighter up above my head to light the first candle my thumb hooked on the extinguisher lever and out it went. I quickly dropped the lighter to the floor, relit the flame and raised it back up to start the process again. By this time the other individual lighting candles was way ahead of me on the top step lighting his last three candles. I quickly navigated through the candle maze, lighting each one on the fly. After lighting the last candle, the two of us now facing each other on opposite sides of the pulpit, turned in unison to step down the stairs on the sides and me, not realizing how close the first step was, I stepped into nothing but air with my left leg and I tumble down 6 steps like I was doing cartwheels. When I stopped rolling, I found myself lying at the feet of my buddy's future mother-in-law and if looks could kill, I would have been dead on the spot.

One year at a variety show I was putting on in The Golden West Main Stage Theater, I was going out to introduce the first act of the show. As I walked out on stage, it was pitch black and the stage lights had not come on yet. As the lights came up, I was already stepping into space with my good leg. I fell off the stage into the orchestra pit, did a front roll and reemerged still holding my microphone and not a wrinkle in my tuxedo. The funny thing is many people in the audience thought I did it on purpose and it was part of the show, and I never tried to dispute their claim.

So as you can see falling down has always been a part of my life. Some greater than others and some more painful than others, but always they ended up strengthening my character.

Philosophies

I have always lived by philosophies that don't just affect my thinking, but benefit my family, friends and fellow man.

The Big Picture-

Knowing that the decisions we make at some point in time can have an influence on other people's lives prompts me to always examine up front, what result my choice will have on others. I never narrow the scope of my decisions based on the outcome for myself or my program. Don't just see the big picture, understand it.

The Need of the Many-

This is what I call my "Star Trek Philosophy". Whenever I make a decision, I want to make sure it is all inclusive of the population it is going to affect. Remember, "The needs of the many outweigh the needs of the few". In other words, if I can't fairly do it for everyone, I'm not going to do it for anyone. People do talk!

Don't ask people to do something you're not willing to do yourself-

I think of all the philosophies I have, this may be the most important. If you have a task that needs to be performed (no matter how menial it may seem) if others know you'll get down and dirty with them, you'll have tremendous support.

Build relationships with everyone-

Every outstanding leader I know builds sincere relationships with everyone they have a working relationship with. If you care about them, they'll care about you. You, as an individual, need to figure out how to achieve this in your environment, but make sure that it does happen.

Share responsibilities don't dictate them-

I love to bring in new employees and discuss with them how I what them to grow as a person as well as a member of staff. In our discussion, we chat about the fact that I want them to feel confident and safe in making decisions. I'll tell them if they come up with an idea or do the work, I'll make sure they get the credit, but if they are willing to take the risk and it doesn't work out, I'll take the blame. If you're not willing to support their decisions, then how can you ever really gain some ones trust?

Make yourself as valuable as possible-

If you are willing to put yourself out there, volunteer when need be, learn as much as you can about your job and the programs that are on your periphery, then you will achieve this goal.

A great example of putting these philosophies in motion happened a few years back when a friend of mine named Steve Tamanaha was working as the supervisor of a major Sothern California landscaping company. He was burnt out and needed a change. I told him to go back to college and earn his Masters Degree in Educational Counseling, and I would hire him to work for me at Golden West College while he was in school. He decided to do it. For the next two years he went to night school and worked for me during the day. I had him learning every aspect of our program as well as interacting with other student services departments on campus and becoming versed in their operations. He became educated in everything from data entry to working directly with students.

One day, I asked him to be the GWC representative on a consortium whose task was to work on blending high school adult education transitional programs with community college programs. He did not question my request and he said he'd do it, but when he went home and told his wife about my request, they both questioned the value.

Three years later, after he had graduated and worked in the field for a year, he was interviewing for a college administrative job similar to mine. The first question the panel asked him was, "Have you ever worked with adult school transitional programs blending into community college?" After the interview, he went home and told his wife about that specific question, and they both just shook their heads.

Oh, by the way, he was one year out of school and he got the job!

True loves

As you know from reading my book, when I got to my college years I finally figured out how to have strong and casual relationships with women. In this part of the book I want to spend some time talking about the three truly special ladies that I've been blessed to have had in my adult life.

First there is Carla. We met at Golden West College in the mid 70's. She was a beautiful blonde woman with a heart of gold. We dated for over a year and decided to get married. It was in our wedding when I fell down going down the aisle. A couple years later we had a son named Earnest Gerald Marchbank IV (Jerry). As wonderful as Carla was to me, within a couple years we realized it wasn't going to work out and we were divorced, sharing custody of our son.

A couple of years later I remarried a stunning and feisty Hispanic women named Cindy. She had a 3 yr. old son named Ryan who immediately brought joy to me as well. A few years later we had a third son together, Garrett. Together we helped raise all three boys into adulthood. After 22 yrs. of marriage we too grew apart and divorced.

These two failed marriages I blame on myself. If you have read this book you know I became very career oriented early on. I put all my drive to prove myself before everything and I know if I would have had better vision on what is truly important, I would still be with Cindy today. Life is funny though because it wasn't until I was hurt at that football game and lost my career that I learned, as good as I was in athletic training, I was still a replaceable cog, but if you're not showing that same dedication to your wife, you're a missing cog and things will change.

Well no matter what happened, both of these lovely women are remarkable and between us we brought up three wonderful loving boys that aren't afraid to walk up and give me a hug and kiss anytime any place. Thanks Carla and Cindy we did good.

After I went back and received my Masters Degree in Counseling, it shed a new light on what is important in my life. I've proved a lot, achieved a lot, and I guess impressed some people along the way, but I needed to learn to put my heart first and put achievements on the back burner. With that new desire a number of years ago, I met a gorgeous mysterious woman that over the next two and a half years became my potential soul mate. My ultimate commitment had become making her strong, trusting and I wanted to light up her life. For me this was a time of ultimate love, the kind of place you only climb to once, but for some reason the romanticism fell away from her heart as she struggled to find herself. Once again I blamed myself for not bringing enough to sustain the relationship.

I know now, that more important than any job, or success, or financial achievement, true love and commitment to a person means the most. Being able to show that you care more about your significant other's needs, than your own, by proving that they're the most important person in the world. You must build their innermost trust by truly listening, and putting their desires first, always before your own.

I have lost much in the past by not having these priorities in place, but I hope God can see his way to give me another chance with the right person, to make them happy for as long as I live.

My boys

As you know I was blessed with three wonderful sons each of them skilled in their own way.

Ryan is insightful, caring, and very loving. He is committed to family first and the rest of the world second. He constantly is concerned about my health and well-being. At a drop of a hat he will be there if you need anything and with his heart of gold he'll make things happen even when it seems impossible.

Jerry is very calculating, he does worry too much about work, but he has his priorities in place with his wife and young son, Earnest Gerald Marchbank V (Jared). He too is always concerned about my health and gets very emotional about any negative medical news that he hears about me. It's nice to know one living Marchbank can openly show emotions and produce tears.

Garrett is much different than his two brothers. He is not reserved and speaks his mind openly to anyone. He is a naturally born leader and people flock to him like a piper. He has wonderful acting skills and a craziness about him that is matched by few in this world, believe me it's true. Although he likes to keep his family life private he too constantly worries about my health.

Besides loving me, the one common thread these three boys share is their concern about my physical well being. I must tell you, it is not about my health deteriorating, it's because I still push the envelope beyond the acceptable limits for a Polio survivor.

AS I CLOSE THIS BOOK,
I LEAVE YOU WITH THIS.

I have achieved a lot in my life, some failures, but many successes. I've been places and seen things that many men can only dream of and I've received awards and achieved accomplishments that to me are mind boggling. None of these achievements would have been possible without many people believing in me along the way. Over time I have been honored many times and I'm always humbled by the experience, but one time stands out from the rest. It happened when my youngest son Garrett was five years old. We were at home and he was playing in the front room and I looked up to see him limping. I went out and said to him "are you alright son?" He looked up at me and said "yea dad, I just want to be like you". I turned around went back in my room and that day I sat down and truly wanted to cry.